Praise for That Th!nk You Do

Without question, the right book at the right time for so many who will look upon this as a mirror, reflecting many situations and circumstances resembling those we've encountered. Stories told with candor and an extraordinary level of honesty, along with advice which becomes the magic elixir we can all draw from as we continue to navigate that unpredictable journey called life.
- *Dennis J. Pitocco, Publisher & Editor-in-Chief, BizCatalyst 360°*

A true polymath, Carrabis blends the astute wisdom of Covey, the practical guidance of Ferriss, and the sagacity of Dear Abby into an eclectic potpourri of advice and opinion. This assortment of insights is a veritable box of chocolates, each one sure to please. Drawing from multiple disciplines—principally psychology, sociology, anthropology, and business—the author shares his unique perspectives. Throughout the chapters covering a wide variety of topics, readers are encouraged to think and behave in new and improved ways.
- *Victor Acquista, M.D., award-winning international author*

I sipped at Joseph Carrabis' That Think You Do. Change, choice, connection, and conversation (inner and outer) make for a hearty brew. Hooked by the exacting sensory images; neuroscience and wit added spice. I stopped often to digest the richness of resonant principles he weaves throughout.

This is a book I'll put on my library shelf and return to again and again.
- *Susan Sneath, co-host of the internet tv talk show "The Change Zone"*

Joseph's vast experiential wisdom and quick wit comes through in this display of poignant and often profound observations of how we can better do what we do, all based on a keen insight and understanding of his own process and success. Few can express and imbue our lives with such eloquent and often humorous deep dives into being a leader of your own business, life and relationships, let alone all the dynamics that entails. His short snippets of a reality which few of us experience in such depth is invigorating to read and ponder. His material demonstrates emotional, intellectual, and even spiritual understanding we often don't consider, let alone embrace and engage in our lives and work. The chapter pieces are quick reads. I highly recommend it for engaging those moments between That Th!nk You Do, too. Enjoy!

    - Zen Benefiel, DD, MA, MBA, TLC, Author, Coach, Educator, Facilitator, Host

Joseph's masterpiece connects science, data, and research with the practicality (and yes complexity) with our everyday lives and how we can begin to better understand what makes us tick (as opposed to being a ticking time bomb!) And all of this is delivered with a strategically delivered sense of humour!

I feel joyfully challenged by Joseph's masterful subtleness to look deeper with clarity at my own habits and am grateful he has provided tools to support the process.

    - Gail McDonald, Executive Coach, TV talk show host - The Change Zone

In this book there are sparks of ideas and thoughts which can be a catalyst for creating positive change in your life. The principles he lives by are seeds to plant for yourself and carry into both your personal and professional life.

    - Eileen Bild, MA, CEO Ordinary to Extraordinary Life, Internationally Syndicated Columnist, Author

Joseph Carrabis

THAT TH!NK YOU DO

60 WAYS TO BE HAPPY, HEALTHY, AND HOLD OFF HARM

Northern Lights Publishing

Nashua, NH

Copyright © 2022 Joseph Carrabis

All rights reserved. No part of this book may be reproduced in any form or by any electronic means, including information storage and retrieval systems, without permission in writing from the publisher, except by reviewers, who may quote brief passages in a review.

Paperback ISBN 978-0-9841403-7-4
epub ISBN 978-0-9841403-8-1
iBook ISBN 978-0-9841403-9-8

Library of Congress Control Number

Characters, events, places, and things described, depicted, or referred to in this work are fictitious. Any similarity to actual persons, events, places, or things is purely coincidental.

Editing by Jennifer Day, Susan Carrabis
Front cover image by John Bernard Scullin
Book design by Jennifer Day

Printed and bound in the United States of America
First printing January 2023

Published by Northern Lights Publishing
www.northernlightspublishing.com

For Susan
(because everything should be)
And AJ
(who said I could)

Special thanks to
Jennifer "JenBitch" Day
who said "We should make a book out of this!"

and

Joseph Della Rosa
who explained *LifeHack* to me

And of course thanks to all the people through the years who asked me to talk, chat, help, guide, and teach.
I doubt I did any of those things, really.
I just helped them find their own doors.

And mostly thanks to my Grandpa
who taught me a variation of Mr. Magorium's
"Life is an occasion, rise to it!"

Note to readers:
You can agree or disagree with anything written here and I offer a suggestion for both:
take a moment to understand and appreciate what causes the agreement and/or disagreement. Such is the beginning of all knowledge.

Contents

Praise for That Th!nk You Do	i
Foreword by Eileen Bild, CEO Ordinary to Extraordinary Life, Internationally Syndicated Columnist and Author	vii
Author's Note	xi
Change (which is Constant) and Managing the Work-Life Balance	1
Taking Back Your Life, part 1	3
Taking Back Your Life, part 2	7
Get a Good Mad Going – It Might Be Good For You	11
Four Rules for Thinking Like An Expert	15
Rewarding Your Critical Actors	19
Can't Be Happy? Blame Your Parents	23
Want to be Heard? See a Musician	27
Want to Kick the Habit? Play Some Music	29
Risky Drinking	33
Marriage Outcrossing	35
Stop Making Babies and Save the Planet	39
Depression Busters, part 1	43
Depression Busters, part 2	47
Birth Control's Long History	51
Avoiding Self-Destructive Behaviors	53
Going It Alone	57
Be Honest with Yourself, Be Honest with Others, Be at Peace	61
Predicting Your Own Future	65
The Liz Effect	67
Did You See What He Was Wearing?	73
Fear of Rejection	75
Take to the Road	81
A 3AM Phone Call	85
The Lady on the Table	91
Unhealthy Comparisons	93
Breaking Up Can Be a Killer and Other Ways to Add/Remove Years from your Life	97

How Do You Define "Love"?	99
What Kind of Lover Are You (And Can You Improve)?	105
Intention	113
Eat Better or Be Stupid, Your Choice	117
No Brain, No Gain (or something like that)	119
Framing Decisions	121
The Stranger The Better	125
Lohginess Begone! (Personal Inventories)	129
Finishing	133
Appendix: Principles	137
Appendix: Definitions	151
Curious about Joseph's fiction?	155
Cymodoce	157
The Goatmen of Aguirra	161
Mani He	167
Coming Soon From Northern Lights Publishing	179
About Northern Lights Publishing	181
Also by Joseph Carrabis	183
About The Author	191
Did you enjoy *That Th!nk You Do*?	193

Foreword by Eileen Bild, CEO Ordinary to Extraordinary Life, Internationally Syndicated Columnist and Author

I have always been a scholar at heart and study cross disciplinary areas such as philosophy, neuroscience, spirituality, psychology, science, and metaphysics. When Joseph Carrabis shared with me his own cross disciplinary studies and brought his knowledge, experience, and insights into book form, I was intrigued. He presents an underlying element of life that is layered with various nuances we can look deeper into separately or in combination, like putting a puzzle together to see the full picture.

Joseph and I met through a mutual friend, and we realized immediately the like-mindedness of the way we view the world. Our unique way of expression and response to experiences enables us to have extended conversations beyond the norm. His sense of humor combined with my free spirit thinking brings an engaging conversation expanding into the crevices of what makes the world go round.

By taking different aspects of life, living, and the balance needed to make it in the world as unscathed as possible, Joseph takes us through his own journey of building an incredible business and the lessons learned along the way. These include the way people think, why they do what they do, living by specific principles, understanding happiness, work-life balance, and his suggestions of how-to's for living life effortlessly and purposefully.

If you ever wonder about how to think like an expert, the difference between your inner critic and the actor within, your ability to be heard, the value of being a musician, how to protect yourself from liars or how to overcome fears, you will find answers in this book.

Through each chapter there is a magic wand taking you into an area of life that you may have experienced yourself or it will be something new to consider. There is synthesis between the known and unknown, the seen and unseen, the mental and the physical, the desires of the heart and the mental mind; and the overall theme of we are just trying to make it from one day to the next with joy, peace, and happiness.

Joseph gives his own insights throughout the pages of what he believes are the backbone of what weaves together to bring us life experiences. Some great, others not so great. He leaves it up to the reader to discern what is true for them. You will find yourself wanting to explore more of each of his analysis of life's nuggets, many of which we create ourselves through questions, desires for specific outcomes and the need to be heard.

I found myself comparing my own life journey and discerning what might be relatable and if I agree with Joseph's interpretation. I believe we are all students of life and when there are tidbits of one's story shared for the sake of giving information that may help others learn, grow, or transform, we are blessed with a gift. It is up to us as to what we do with this gift.

I recommend reading through the book once, coming back through with notebook in hand jotting down the highlights. Then one at a time, research for more information of what you may not know much about. You may find some dots connecting and puzzle pieces come together over time. In this book there are sparks of ideas and thoughts which can be a catalyst for creating positive change in your life. The principles he lives by are seeds to plant for yourself and carry into both your personal and professional life.

Eileen Bild, MA
CEO Ordinary to Extraordinary Life
Founder of OTEL Universe, A Universal Voice
Founder of The Core Thinking Blueprint Method
Breakthrough S.P.A.R.K. Coach
Internationally Syndicated Columnist, Author
www.oteluniverse.com, www.corethinkingblueprint.com

Author's Note

These chapters originally appeared between 2008 and 2016 as blog posts on my That Think You Do blog. My work and research covered a number of fields, my work was recognized in many of them, and much of that appeared as these blog posts.

The language used in this book may offend some readers. My goal is to use all the tools at an author's disposal and all the tools in my author's toolbag to create as exacting a sensory experience for the reader and to be as accurate to my creation as possible. Sometimes that means language which may offend some is used to create such exacting sensory images. I've learned to accept my limitations and hope you'll do the same.

Characters, events, places, and things described, depicted, or referred to in this work are fictitious. Any similarity to actual persons, events, places, or things is purely coincidental.

Please be aware this book is not a substitute for professional and medical help. I am not a mental health professional, and nothing in this book is intended to diagnose or treat illness of any kind. If you are

currently in distress or crisis, please put this book down immediately and find assistance. Here are some US-based places to start:
- National Suicide Prevention Hotline: 1-800-273-TALK (8255)
- Veteran's Crisis Line: 1-800-273-8255, press 1
- Emergency Medical Services: Call 911
- Substance Abuse and Mental Health Services Referral Helpline for general mental health information and to locate treatment services in your area: 1-877-SAMHSA7 (726-4727)
- FindTreatment.gov
- MentalHealth.gov

Non US-based readers are encouraged to reach out to organizations in their local communities.

THAT TH!NK YOU DO

60 WAYS TO BE HAPPY, HEALTHY, AND HOLD OFF HARM

*"Be so confident in knowing what you bring to
the table you're willing to eat alone until you find the right table."*

Change (which is Constant) and Managing the Work-Life Balance

Susan (wife, partner, all things known and unknown) and I are coming on our 25th wedding anniversary. (note to readers: we just celebrated our 38th) We've been together for 31 years (now 44). I wrote our wedding vows:

I can not promise you fidelity, sanity, health, hope, love, comfort or joy. All I can promise is that I will change. Not all my changes will be good. I ask God's help that not all will be bad.

I ask you today to be with me in my changes, to tell me when I am foolish, to heal me when I am sick, to love me when I forget to love, to give me hope when I have none to give, to give me comfort when I am cold and alone, to give me joy when all I know is sadness.

Stand with me the rest of my days. I have asked you to do this. I ask you again, here, before our friends and families. It is said before others, but the words are for you. I love you.

Nobody in the audience knew what the vows would be, not even the minister. People knew I'd written them and everyone assumed they'd be whimsical if not funny. I can't tell you the number of people who've asked for copies of our vows since then.

What is saddest is that of the 80 couples who attended (and barring deaths) only two couples remain as couples. Death took only two other couples.

Why did we last as a couple? Perhaps because we defined our relationship from the beginning by the changes we would go through — both known and unknown — and recognizing that nothing is static, everything evolves.

Study change, study evolution, and you learn that nature preserves balance of the whole at great cost. Nature reshapes oceans and continents, moves galaxies and suns, creates light and darkness in equal measure, and always to keep itself in balance, a mobile of eternity sent singing a balance of harmonies by the winds of change.

Isn't it then a demonstration of whatever gods one honors to give the Universe rest by keeping oneself in as much balance as possible?

Want to know how to weather the times, economic upheavals, business successes and failures, the birth of a child and the loss of a friend? Keep yourself in balance first with yourself then with the world around you. Spend as much time fostering yourself as you do others, give as much time to others as you do yourself. Your world can change in less than a heartbeat so do joy whenever you can. The world will take care of bringing you sorrow when you least expect it.

The bad news is that keeping yourself in balance is in itself a full time job. It is what you were really born to do. Get used to it. Recognize it. Do it. The good news is that making keeping yourself in balance your full time job means everything else falls into place faster than you can imagine, in less than a heartbeat, when you least expect it, so take joy in it.

Taking Back Your Life, part 1

People often share with me they feel overwhelmed, that their life is out of control, that there are too many demands and not enough time. These feelings aren't unique and are increasingly common in our information-rich world. Let me share some simple things neuroscience tells us can help us get our lives back under control. In this section I'll share some things I do personally, and later I'll share things I've found helpful when necessary.

Be Average, Be Simple

I make lists. Gosh, do I make lists. Some stay in my head and most of them get down on paper. A few go onto the computer and even then they might stay on paper. Anyway, perhaps, like me, lists are helpful to you. I learned to make lists by starting with simple ones. I wrote down only two things, made them easy to do and rewarded myself for doing them. The rewards were also simple. One reward I still use is simply stopping what I'm doing, taking a deep breath, closing my eyes and letting myself relax into my chair for about a minute. If you're thinking this doesn't sound like much, you're absolutely correct — it's nothing at all. What this comes down to is there's no reason for you to not do it and every reason to go ahead and do it.

Stay on Track

The list provides my goals. Next I put down a start time and how long I think it will take to accomplish (and I pad the time involved liberally). I don't write down a stop time and there's a reason for that. What I do write down is a break time and how long my breaks will be (I also pad this liberally). I use these break times to evaluate my progress (I'm gentle with myself), and (very important!) I decide if the goal is still worth achieving. The challenge (for me, anyway) is being honest with myself. I know from my studies that recognizing I've outgrown a goal is a sign of maturity and wisdom, not failure, and continuing to focus on something I no longer value is foolishness. Sometimes I just don't feel like being mature and wise, though, and that's a real sign I need a break (don't you think?).

Overwhelm Me Not!

Sometimes I feel overwhelmed by everything on my plate. That feeling — more than anything else — is a signal I have to objectively look at my list. I find out what task I'm supposed to be working on right then. Then I take a moment to balance and center myself, take a deep breath then go back to the task at hand.

When It's Done, It's Done

I keep my list with me. My personal choice is 3x5 index cards, a habit I got into when I was a teenager (ask me about studying with Master Logician John Leslie sometime). I don't use a smartphone or some such because the act of writing on an index card helps me to remember. I have a separate index card for each task. This allows me to conceptualize and view each task separately.

Two things come from this. One, I'm not going back to the same well for each task. Two, being able to "tear up" the card when the task is done is (for me) gratifying. That second part is a biggie: it's a definite sign and demonstration that that task is completed, over, done with. Yeeha, time to celebrate (and I do). If nothing else, physically carrying a tasklist with you allows you to check things off when they're done. And when they're done, they're done. I can always come up with ways to make a completed task better (so clever, me. I love to make work for myself, don't you?) and when I do it becomes a new item on the list, not a reopening of a completed task. Few things are as cognitively exhausting as thinking you're done with something then having to go back to it again and again and again.

Successful Multitaskers are Serialtaskers

I prioritize my tasks and recognize my limits, a kind of "Task A is my main task and I know when I'm tired of it I can do less demanding tasks B and C. Then once I get tired of them I can go back to task A refreshed." I group tasks that require different skills in my day. For example, let's take task A as doing financials. Task B might be answering 2-3 emails and task C might be checking in with a co-worker via the phone. The important item in these three tasks is that they utilize (hence exhaust) different mental skills. Exhaust one mental skill, give that part of your brain a rest and spend some time on a completely different type of task. Multitasking - I started by limiting myself to three things at a time and discovered I was much more productive. When I could handle three tasks easily I added a fourth and so on. Now consider the figure above. Notice that task 1 stops before task 2 starts and so on? That's because few (very few!) people can truly do more than one thing at a time. What they do is time-slice. They do one thing then another, then go back to the former and so on. The trick is to recognize what are interruptions and what truly deserves your attention. Interruptions that truly require your attention are called *meaningful noise* and are a study in themselves. So when I multitask I'm really serialtasking and I congratulate myself for each task I spend time on. Sometimes it's just a glass of water, a cup of coffee or a walk outside. Again, this reward is for spending time on a task, not just completing it. I decided a long time ago to take back control of my life.

Maybe some of the above will work for you, as well. Next I will share six simple things neuroscience tells us can help people take back control of their life.

Taking Back Your Life, part 2

The whole key to taking back control of your life is allowing yourself to feel good about yourself. I'm surprised at how few people have this ability any more. Being pulled in many different directions often only serves to pull us off balance, to cause us to forget who we are and why we're doing what we do.

Personal Philosophy Alert: We're here for each other.

For what it's worth and (hopefully) for your pleasure and enlightenment, here are six more simple ways neuroscience and psychology tell us we can take back control of our lives.

Decide If It's Worth the Effort

Is something upsetting you? Take a moment to decide if what's upsetting you is worth the energy and effort you're devoting to it. Chances are what's upsetting you is out of your control, isn't what you think it is, is a miscommunication, and so on. You can laugh or rage at what happens in your life and either one can leave you in tears and gasping for breath. Given the options, putting the energy into laughter makes your heart and mind stronger.

Take Time to Play

Staring at the computer waiting for something to load, someone to arrive, an email to be returned, does nothing but increase your blood pressure. Really, do you feel good about it? So play when you have to wait for something to happen. My choice? The guitar, clarinet, or piano. I know some people who are wizards at solitaire or keep a good book handy. Little moments of play in the middle of busy days keeps your mind alert, your emotions on keel, and allows you to focus when you do get back.

Recognize When You've Had Enough

This is an amplification of #2 and can be thought of as "Know when to stop." Sometimes simple discussions can get out of hand and the reasons aren't always obvious. Take a moment to get yourself out of the moment (so to speak) and analyze what's going on. Maybe it's time to take a break. This applies to discussions, work groups, house chores, anything and everything. A reframe of this is "It's okay to get tired and take a little rest." Lots of people will work or talk or think beyond their internal exhaustion point then get frustrated at the poor results, so recognize when you've had or done enough, stop for a while and come back later, refreshed.

Stretch or Move Whether You Need to or Not

Our bodies and minds weren't designed to work in offices or in small spaces. Given enough time, they'll rebel in one way or another and usually the end result is not good. When you start to feel signs of mental fatigue, get up. Walk. Stretch. Get some one, five or ten pound weights and keep them under your desk (or whatever). Are you on the phone a lot? Do curls or tricep extensions while you talk. Stand up and touch your toes while waiting for a program to load or an email to open.

Slow Down

More and more people are becoming slaves to their digital servants. Part of this modern malaise is that people can't keep up with all the demands coming at them from their email, their cellphones, their this and their that. I know the old adage "Never put off 'till tomorrow what you can do today" and let me offer a healthier alternative "The world can't end today because it's already tomorrow in Australia" (I know the reframe loses something for Ozian readers). Increased interconnectivity is creating an unhealthy interdependence that we are designed to deal with neither effectively nor efficiently, so learn to recognize what's truly important. You might end up in digital remission. It's a happy place to be.

Drink More Water

I laughed at this until I started doing it. Lots of people hit their wall mid-afternoon and usually get a cup of coffee. Drink a glass of water instead. Usually our bodies are busy digesting our lunches by mid-afternoon and go into a mild dehydration state. A glass of pure water (then a cup of coffee if you must) allows our metabolisms to balance.

The whole key to everything here is to decide (yes, you must decide or at least become aware that you can make the decision) if you feel good about what you're doing. If you don't, ask yourself why you're doing it. If there's no goodness involved, stop it.

I mean, really ... you do want to be in control of your life, don't you?

Get a Good Mad Going – It Might Be Good For You

You're about to enter a meeting and you've been warned you're going to be challenged ... a lot.

Is it better

- to seek a quiet place, to calm yourself, to find your center and go into the meeting relaxed or
- to focus on the idea of being challenged, being put on the spot, possibly being singled out in front of your peers?

Based on studies performed in Boston and elsewhere, it's better to enter confrontational situations a little hot under the collar.

Just so we're clear on things, I'm not suggesting you go in armed for bear and looking to take no prisoners, nothing of the sort.

That offered, chances are you'll come out of the meeting or situation better if you go in with your blood up. The reasons are (evolutionary-wise) simple. Knowing a confrontation or some unpleasantness will take place gives your mind and body and evolutionary advantage, the "fight" aspect of what use to be called the flight-or-fight response. Just knowing a challenge is looming causes changes to your body chemistry, especially your neural chemistry. You go from prey to predator mode, essentially, and your body adjusts itself without your realizing it's doing so. Your movements, your voice, your expressions, even your irises start giving off "Keep your distance, bucko!" signals that other people, equally without realizing it, pick up and respond to.

Walk Like a ... Predator

Long ago I taught women's self-defense and there was very little combat technique involved. What I did teach them was how to walk like a predator — on their toes — without obviously walking on their toes. Why walk like a predator? Because when you're giving off "predator" signals it's very difficult for others to consider you prey.

In addition to toe-walking, keep your eyes forward, look from side to side by moving your whole head. Tilt your head slightly forward (and keep your neck straight up from your shoulders). Blink as seldom as possible and open your eyes wide without being obvious about it. Walk with your hands empty and open, palms towards your body, elbows just slightly bent. Match your breathing to your movements and remember to relax.

Synchronize your large body movements — swinging the arms and legs — so your motion is both smooth and effortless (this is good regardless as any Alexander or Feldenkrais practitioner will tell you). Predators conserve energy until they need it and this style of walking shows that conservation in action.

The kicker is flaring your nostrils. Really. Flared nostrils are one of the most primitive aggression displays humans possess. The next time you're being bothered by someone — like at a meeting, just in conversation, on the subway or something — stare at them, don't blink, and flare your nostrils. Not obviously so, just enough. They'll excuse themselves or find someone else to harass without knowing why they want to get away. In the very least they'll ask if everything's okay without knowing what they're really asking about.

Next time we're at a conference together ask me to demonstrate it for you. When you know what I'm doing it's pretty funny to watch.

Four Rules for Thinking Like An Expert

What is expertise? Most people know it when they see it or when they're in the presence of someone with expertise in a given field. Talking with a friend yesterday, she admitted she hardly feels like an expert even though she's taught at the university level. "How come?" "Because I'm old enough to know what I don't know," she answered. So I invited her to play a game with me and here I share it with you. It's very simple, and is something you can do on your own in very little time each and every day. In the end, people will consider you an expert even if you don't think that's true yourself.
1. Pick a subject or topic that fascinates you, something you like, something that genuinely gets your heart pounding and your mind working. It doesn't matter what the subject or topic is, all that matters is it interests you. The reason is simple: your enthusiasm will keep you on track towards recognizable expertise. Have something picked out? Good.

2. Start writing down patterns and similarities. All things repeat over time. Sometimes the time involved is eons and sometimes it's tenths of a second. What is important is that you note when and how patterns start and stop, begin and end. Notice what appears to be the end of a pattern? Know how long these things take to start again? Congratulations. You can predict when it will happen again. Now you're an expert. In addition to patterns, write down similarities. Do all male movie stars tend to buy the same clothes or shop at the same stores? See one wearing something new and now you can predict what will be the fashion rave for that year.
3. Organize what you know. Once you've recognized patterns and similarities it's time to organize them into blocks of knowledge. Pick out a few "big" or "obvious" features of your favorite subject or topic. Now organize (or block together) all the little or less obvious features that accompany those big and obvious features. The next time you encounter a bunch of those smaller features blocked together you can announce the "big" thing that's happening that nobody else has noticed and again, voila, you're an expert.
4. Stick to your chosen subjects. The quickest way to be recognized as an expert in some field is to be repeatedly correct about what's going on in that field. Likewise, the quickest way to be considered incompetent in a given field is to make mistakes about what's going on in that field. So once you're recognized in one field, keep yourself current in that field then repeat the process again with a second field. The crucial hint here is to make your secondary subjects closely related to your first. Kind of like being recognized as an expert chef, then becoming known as an expert on seasonings, then on cooking utensils and so on.

Some things are easy, some things are hard. Some things, like being recognized as an expert, simply take a little practice. Go tell your friends about this technique and maybe you'll be recognized as being an expert on being an expert.

Rewarding Your Critical Actors

Do you have a little voice inside your head that warns you about things you're about to do? Maybe it goes beyond warning you, perhaps it out and out chides you or even yells so loudly it stops you dead in your tracks?

Congratulations, you've been in touch with what people studying learning models call your *critic* (not a surprising name considering what it does, is it?).

Do you have a little voice inside your head that makes suggestions on how to get the most out of whatever you're about to do? Maybe it goes beyond suggestions, maybe it reminds you of what worked and what didn't in the past? Maybe it demands this path be followed over that path?

Congratulations again, now you're talking with your *actor*.

Want to learn how to confuse them or even shut them up completely? It's probably obvious (once you think about it) that our mind's actor and critic come from different parts of the brain. The critic comes from the front part of the brain where reasoning occurs, the actor from the rear of the brain where we process vision and memory (generally speaking).

Both are necessary. They're part of what's called *instrumental conditioning* and constitute the most basic form of *adaptive behavior*. Adaptive behavior and instrumental conditioning are very important to our survival as individuals and as a species. We adapt how we behave in order to maximize rewards and minimize punishments, and that process of adapting is done in (hopefully) small steps by conditioning ourselves to our environment.

The actor reminds us what happened before in similar environments and helps us predict what to do in the present environment. The critic predicts future gains and losses by evaluating present conditions and information out of our direct experience. We need both of them. They work in tandem for most of us and people lacking one or the other tend to take unnecessary risks or avoid new situations altogether.

But what if your critic-actor is too critical or too … umm … actorial?

Both critic and actor cause the brain to send hormonal signals through the body. Most often these signals are survival oriented — great for the jungle and possibly night walks in a city, not quite the same as deciding what you should purchase or whether or not to get on that really big roller coaster.

So here's how to deal with both and let you — your hopefully rational, thinking, intelligent self — make the decisions.

First, Agree

People think this is an odd suggestion and it comes from lots of studies. When your critic is saying "No, don't! Danger, Will Robinson! Danger!" respond with "Thanks. That's good advice. I appreciate your letting me know that" or something similar. Strangely enough, all the critic really wants to know is that you're paying attention to warning signs in the environment. Letting your critic know you're doing so is often enough to either shut it up or quiet it down, at least for a while. Similarly, agree with your actor. Same rules apply.

Second, Take a Deep Breath

Remember those hormonal signals I mentioned? Those signals are survival based, as in fight or flight. Taking a deep breath, centering yourself, maybe even closing your eyes for a second, all send counter-signals telling your brain and body "It's okay. You can relax now. I'm here." Think of something funny, a joke or some such. Put a smile on your face. A real smile, not just a polite one. You'll find you can think clearer when you do.

Third, Act Intentionally

Your critic and actor are exerting all sorts of energy to tell you what might, possibly could, or should happen. The truth is neither they nor you know what will happen. What you do know is what's happening right "now" in the moment of the decision. This is where you take control of your adaptive learning and instrumental conditioning to your own best benefit. Decide what option looks best "as far as the eye can see" so to speak and make a deal with your actor and critic. Ask them to cover your back and let you know if something needs your attention. Nothing quiets these primitive parts of the mind more than asking them to help. Seriously.

Lastly, Take Small Steps

You've chosen a path, now move in that direction. Just a little, not a lot. Are you still okay? Everything still good? Great. Lather, Rinse, Repeat. The moment you can't see what's going on or things stop being okay, back up to your last safe spot and decide if you want to continue or not.

Summary

Your actor and critic are there for a reason. The goal is to use them rather than letting them abuse you.

Enjoy.

That Th!nk You Do! by Joseph Carrabis

Can't Be Happy? Blame Your Parents

Are you happy? Do you have a positive outlook on life? Is the glass usually half full when you drink from it?

If so, there's a better than even chance you're from Latin American countries, possibly the US and could have northern Mediterranean ancestry. Not so happy? Chances are your from Asia or the Pacific Rim countries.

What ... did you think I was going to suggest you blame your parents for your outlook on life? Maybe in another column, but this time out we're going to look at how ethnic origins — ancestry — often pre-determines how you'll deal with life's situations big and small.

According to a now long-standing study involving five dominant ethnic groups, ethnic origins play a significant role in how people view their world. These results don't surprise me, and I'm sure they don't surprise anyone with a cultural anthropology background.

But why is one culture happier than another? Cultures that place higher values on self-worth and self-fulfillment — as opposed to group identity — tend to promote happier, psychologically healthier individuals. But wait, there's more ...

It also seems that cultures that promote open emotionalism have happier, psychologically healthier individuals.

Open emotionalism? Yes. As in crying when you're sad, laughing when you're happy, talking about your feelings with others, showing and sharing your disappointments and anger, getting hot under the collar when appropriate (see "Get a Good Mad On - It Might Be Good For You" for more on this), ... , recognizing that emotions are the basis of who we are so we might as well share them.

Why self versus group?

Cultures that value individual achievement (regardless of how the culture defines it) over group achievement have happier individuals. The group achievement concept goes back to group dynamics and will be obvious to anyone who's studied 12-Step and similar programs — no one can be healthier than the group is healthy. This is true in groups, tribes, families, and yes you guessed it, societies and cultures. The individual who grows beyond the needs of the program is usually ostracized by others staying in the program. This is completely understandable in recovery programs as they get their strength by their group unity. Individuals electing to leave these programs due to their own growth threaten the group's unity and identity and so it goes.

Ah, but that culture who salutes and honors the hero, the individual who selects a truly unique path and finds joy from it? How can you not be happy when you're honored and respected simply by being the best you possible?

And that Open Emotionalism thing?

The parts of our brains that work at birth, at death, and all times in between are the emotional centers, what is sometimes called the primitive or reptile brain. Some cultures inculcate their members with the belief that emotions are negative and that only logic and reason should be displayed (and Mr. Spock went completely freakin' nuts once every seven years because he had to let his ... emotions ... out, remember?).

What's amusing about that kind of cultural belief is that 1) "belief" in and of itself is emotional in nature and 2) the worst thing one can do for their psychological health is have different parts of their psyche in conflict with each other. It doesn't matter who you are, the primitive brain will win out. It's far better to work with it than attempt to hide, destroy, or ignore it.

So a happy camper? Go ahead and blame your parents. Or at least where they came from. It has a lot to do with it.

Want to be Heard? See a Musician

Do you ever wish someone would just listen to you? That you could find someone who could understand not just the words but the emotions behind them? Well, it turns out that's very easy to do. First, find a musician. If not a musician, someone who's had a great deal of music in their life. From an early age. The earlier the better, in fact. At least that's what researchers at Northwestern University are saying. Or singing. Studies show that people with musical backgrounds from an early point in their lives are wired differently than those without that musical background. Especially those who played music or sang, not just passively listened. People — both males and females and regardless of culture — with music in their blood are much better at detecting and responding to the subtleties in our voices that indicate stress, anxiety, worry, doubt, fear ... hopefully we don't need musical training to recognize and respond to positive emotions in someone's voice.

This auditory advantage takes another form with some of us: if we had lots of sounds in our childhood we can decode the sounds of speech better and faster than those of us who came from quiet families. I'll admit this information makes lots of sense to me. I well remember sitting in my grandmother's kitchen and having the extended family — I think there would be about thirty of us at a whack — sitting and standing around the table, conversations in Italian and English going back and forth, back and forth, some people eating, a couple of uncles and aunts singing, Uncle Freddie playing guitar in the living room, Uncle Louie singing while Cousin Rosalind played piano, … , the sounds were rich and full in my childhood.

A natural ability fostered by such an environment is being able to quickly recognize and decode important information from all the background noise, hence the ability to recognize and decode speech from noise.

So if you happen to visit your partner's family and walk away thinking, "my goodness … do those people ever shut up?" Be grateful. Chances are you're with someone who'll really pay attention when you talk.

And in any case, the next time you really want to be heard, go see a musician.

Even better, if you want to be a good listener, learn to play some music.

Want to Kick the Habit? Play Some Music

If you've read other chapters, you know I've been studying how sounds affect people. This is known as psychophysics and more directly, psycho-acoustics. It's fascinating stuff.

For example, did you know that the parts of the brain that respond to music are involved in the response mechanisms to addictive substances and behaviors?

The evidence comes from various brain-scanning technologies (PET, fMRI, etc) and targeted drug therapies.

And it gets a little better, too. Not only abuse drugs, but it seems these neuronal circuits also are involved in our enjoyment of food and sex.

Food, sex and music.

Reminds me of Yasgur's Farm. *(the location of the original Woodstock Music and Art Fair, (the real one!) if you didn't know. I didn't! -ed.)*

Seriously, there's a reason responses to food, sex, abuse drugs and music all occur in similar brain areas. Imagine yourself as an amoeba in the primordial slime a few billion years ago. There were only two things you really wanted to do: eat and replicate. In fact, there wasn't much about your primitive biology that was geared to doing anything else. Not only your primitive biology but the primitive biologies of every other living organism that was going to survive, these were extremely important and because they were, you and your kind survived.

A few million years go by. You're multi-cellular. You might even be swimming in some ocean and getting ready to traipse across some land. There's really only two reasons you'd want to do that. First, there might be food. Second, there might be someone cute.

Food and sex still rule.

Many million more years go by. Many, many. You're walking around on the land now and you might still be swimming. You might be flying or gliding. In all cases, your mobility is a function of your need to eat — find food — and reproduce — find yourself a cutie. These two functions have taken on such importance to both your and your species' survival that your brain has started to do things to get your attention when you eat or mate. It started to develop some reward circuitry and about the only time it fires is when you're doing things that directly ensure both your and your species' survival.

Food and sex again. Only now we're getting rewarded in new ways for our efforts.

Lots more millions of years go by. You've done well. There are so many of your species now that in order to reproduce you have to demonstrate that you're better than your peers. How might you do that? Evolution comes up with a way. Originally your flopping around or flapping your wings or clapping your flippers happened by accident but it still made potential mates look your way rather than at your peers. Given eons those accidental sounds became intentional mating calls, tweets, splashes, and flaps.

Then we started adding rhythms so that potential mates would be able to pick our grunts and groans out of the crowd.

Then we started howling and calling. That's how music was born.

And the ones of us who made the best music got the most reward.

It's those reward circuits that drugs of abuse fire. The same ones that got us standing up on our hind legs and reading these words rather than dying off millennia ago.

Knowing their origins, it's not odd at all that food, sex, abuse drugs and music go together, is it?

So if you really want to kick the habit, learn to play some music. Food, sex, and drugs are sometimes recognized as addiction vectors in our society. Not so with music. Not yet.

Risky Drinking

There's evidence that people who drink regularly are more prone to risk-taking behavior.

No surprise, correct? You drink, you get behind the wheel of a car, that's a risk. Things like that, right?

True and that's not what I'm writing about. It seems that people who drink — especially people who started drinking young — are more likely to engage in risk-taking behaviors, period. They don't need to be sipping right now to take risks right now, it's if they regularly drink then they regularly take risks regardless of their state of inebriation.

This kind of surprises me. I'm curious to know if the definition of "risk-taking behavior" is the psychology lab standard or not. For example, I grew up in a family that had wine on the table for most meals. I didn't always drink wine with my meals and sometimes did. I think I had my first beer (didn't like it) when I was in my early teens and didn't touch hard liquors until I was in my mid-30s.

People tell me I'm incredibly courageous. This means I do things they wouldn't think of doing. To them, I take risks. To me, I don't.

For example, I don't play cards for money even though I usually win. I don't drive fast (I'm that old fart you can't wait to pass on the highway). Probably the most "dangerous" thing I do is fly my kites (one has a 15m sail, so they're on the large size and can easily lift me off the ground). Even in business I prefer not to take risks.

Once again, Joseph is out beyond the 2db of the study.

But I have observed enough people in enough different cultures to accept that some cultures in which alcoholic beverages are readily available tend to be more accepting of risk-taking behavior — in business, in life, in romance.

I wonder if the greater social net of these other cultures contributes more to a willingness to take risks than does the early availability of alcohol.

And regardless, the evidence is out there. I'd like to suggest that you watch how much your potential partner imbibes and take that as a cue for future financial safety or not, but I can't. There are really too many other factors involved (in my opinion).

So let's put this one on the shelf for a while, something to come back to down the road. And I'd love to know your experiences on this subject.

Marriage Outcrossing

I've been reading some fascinating research this past week. It deals with how mate selection and marriage partnerships have changed in the US in the past fifty years.

It seems that my generation (late boomer) was the last generation to seek partners within tightly conformed cultural boundaries.

That's a fancy way of writing that I "didn't look too far" for a mate. In fact, my generation rarely looked beyond the confines of the college campus. A few years earlier (and discounting war brides) people didn't look too far beyond their high school or town. Back a little further and people didn't look far beyond their neighborhoods.

There are other factors at work in this. What western and some eastern and most modern, non-theocratic cultures recognize as "romantic" love didn't exist until about 1860 in the US and wasn't well established in middle-class Europe, Canada, and the US until about the 1920s (two generations).

Prior to that it was marriage of convenience, for political advantage, to strengthen business empires, blood ties, appeasement, …

My generation is probably the last US-based generation that sought out life-mates that basically looked like the people we grew up with. Times change, they do. Immigrant waves came first to fill the bottom of the economic ladder then prosperous immigrants came and entered directly into higher rungs on that ladder. Educational opportunities changed. Travel became extremely affordable.

And then the horrible thing happened ... one of us married someone who didn't look like us. Think *Guess Who's Coming to Dinner* gone large.

What makes things different now is that the coming generations (again, barring unforeseen circumstances) will be bringing home people who think like them rather than look like them. They will be bringing into their homes people with similar beliefs but beliefs that have nothing to do with creed and credo and instead deal with goals and dreams.

Whatever causes it, it is known as "outcrossing", looking for mates outside of your self-recognized group. The love of my life is neither Catholic nor Italian-American, however she is a brilliant and beautiful woman ... whom I met in college and who comes from a similar socio-economic background. Educational and socio-economic boundaries were my generation's outcrossing boundaries. Stepping over ethnic and religious boundaries were about as outcrossed as my generation could get.

Think about couples you know. Barring war-brides (as noted above), starting from the oldest couples to the youngest, you'll probably notice mates chosen from farther and farther afield (this has been going on in the EU and Canada for much longer than in the US primarily due to cultural differences).

And there's an interesting note about war brides that comes out of this research. Have you noticed that the latest US conflicts (say 1990 forward) are resulting in fewer and fewer war brides? And more properly "war spouses"?

It has to do with more and more women being "on the ground" in these combat environments than in the past.

It's going to be a very brave new world.

Stop Making Babies and Save the Planet

Most readers know I'm a cross-disciplinary, translational researcher. What ... you didn't know that?

Well ... let me give you an idea of what it means ... I read in and study a very wide variety of sciences. I've studied and taught mathematics, history, linguistics, anthropology, physics, religion, ethics, virology ... the list is pretty long. That's the "cross disciplinary" part.

Almost everything I study and read goes into my research and that research often moshes some collection of unrelated sciences, synthesizes them into a working whole then "translates" the working whole into something productizable. That's the "translational" part.

So sometimes in my research I come across something that crosses lots of disciplinary boundaries.

Like something that links a declining or at least stabilized birth rate to a decrease in pollution.

And it makes complete sense.

It's amazingly simple, really. An ongoing and static planetary population equals a static pollution production level (technologic changes aside). This means the amount of pollution may rise while the rate of the rise in pollution levels remains constant rather than rising. "We'll still be killing ourselves, simply not as quickly" is one way to look at it.

Let me give you an every day example: You're driving a car. Let's say you stop at a traffic light. The light changes and you accelerate, and you keep your foot steady on the gas pedal. Because you're accelerating the car travels faster and faster.

Your speed is rising but the rate your speed rises doesn't.

Normally when you reach your desired speed, you ease up on the gas pedal (you don't apply as much pressure, the car stops accelerating and remains at a steady pace (kind of like cruise control)) and the car maintains its speed (doesn't speed up, doesn't slow down).

You're still moving, simply not as quickly as if you kept your foot down on the gas pedal.

Now back to birth rates and such.

Fewer births per million people - a decreasing population - equals a decrease in the production of pollution (this is the "easing up on the gas pedal" part). This can be a very good thing if we haven't reached a climatic tipping point (driving so fast we lose control of the car), not a good thing if we have reached that tipping point because one could then say "We'll still be killing ourselves, it's just going to take a lot longer" (we're still driving too fast, think we can handle it but can't, and doom is waiting at the next bump in the road).

What few people seem to recognize is that it really doesn't matter where one gets their energy, any technology that produces power — nuclear fission, nuclear fusion, solar, wind, geothermal, petroleum-based, fossil-based, ... — is going to have some kind of pollution associated with it. Some will show up relatively quickly (see something coming out of a smoke stack or exhaust pipe? That "quick") and some over millennia (nuclear half-lives, that kind of thing).

But right now humankind is literally at a point where it can pick its poison (slow death or a quick one).

Me? Speaking translationally and cross-disciplinarily, I'm going with the "stop making babies" option because while I may be stupid enough to ruin my life, I sure in heck don't want to ruin some one else's.

You?

Depression Busters, part 1

I know a fellow who is (probably) clinically depressed. His story is sad and, in my experience, typical.

A good worker, he's out of work. Because he specialized, it's not easy to find work. He could do general work and that wouldn't begin to pay his bills.

His life-partner and he go through up times and down times. He and she are different style thinkers (left-right, that kind of thing). Normally this makes them a good team and when the sides go into conflict, they really go into conflict.

She is the bread-winner and although he sometimes throws a haunch of venison on the table, it isn't often enough to sustain them, only a cause for celebration when it occurs.

Just enough good happens to keep him moving forward. He might be called a hoper or a dreamer by some, stupid and stubborn by others.

The number of people suffering depression in the US is kind of fluid. What kind of "depression" are we concerned with? How "depressed"? Clinically? Mild? Probably a safe number is 10%. That's not a large number in some ways. If 10% are depressed, 90% are not depressed.

But is that 90% full of happy, smiling people? Are they content? Or are they just getting by?

I credit people who have enough training to recognize they're depressed. I also realized that being able to recognize depression is most often the result of either being hospitalized or counseled for depression, so one of the best ways to recognize you're depressed is to have been so depressed you needed help.

That's depressing.

Depression Busters

The following are ways to deal with depression. I'm not a doctor, these are suggestions, things that I've seen work, have worked for me, have worked for others who told me they worked, ...

Feel free to give as many a go as you'd like.

- One of the best (my opinion) cures for depression is exercise, preferably in sunshine, preferably with others. Go walk around a park some afternoon, stop and talk with people. Ask them how they're doing. These seemingly minor activities cause different brain areas to work, not to mention pumping endorphins into your system.
- Can't get to a park or go for a neighborhood walk? Go to your town library, pick out a chair, a book, and read.
- Close to the library idea is signing up for a class or study group. Book stores often support this kind of activity in the hopes you'll purchase a book or two for your studies.
- Another excellent strategy is to recognize the things that depress you and avoid them. One thing that happens in depression is that our psychological defenses decline, followed quickly by our physical defenses. People can be quite raw when they're depressed, like an insect molting and having to wait for its new shell to harden, but the depression doesn't allow the

new shell to harden.

The result is things that once made you laugh or you could ignore now become major events. A natural (and me thinks poor) defense against these things is sleep. Sometimes people sleep long and take frequent naps because they're tired, sometimes because their mind needs to work something out and frequent naps give it the time to do so.

But frequent naps when one is depressed is a sign things are getting worse. Yes, naps allow one to avoid whatever is causing the depression but they don't allow one to get new things into their mind to psychologically fight the depression.

- Talk, ultimately, and with someone who actively listens and accepts (as opposed to judges and corrects) is the best. One of depression's hallmarks is the sense of being overwhelmed and out of control of one's own life. Talking with someone who cares and accepts without judging allows you to get some perspective, to find order and put things in their place.

Depression Busters, part 2

Part one offered five basic depression busters. I wrote these because a friend is going through a depressive episode and I recognize that if one person's getting dragged down, there's probably others, hence the suggestions I gave to one I'm making available to all.

Here are six more depression busters, slightly more "aggressive" than the last.

As I wrote before, these are suggestions. Please consult a physician because I'm no expert on these things.

Six More Depression Busters
- Take time to center yourself. Ask yourself "Does this affect me now?" You may be worrying about things that won't happen soon if at all. Another way to ask yourself this same question is "Am I okay now?" Nine times out of ten the answer is "Yes, I am", so just for this second stop worrying, stop being depressed and focus on the fact that right this second you're okay. This is called centering or being in the moment. Now

lather-rinse-repeat. You'll soon discover you're okay for two seconds in a row and now you're on your way.
- Make a List of things to get done. This is something I've written about before in "Taking Back Your Life". Make a simple list of what you need to get done and stick to it. Make it a simple list with easily doable things. Make it two to three simple things long. Such a list gives you successes. It provides a visual demonstration that you can get things done, that you can function. Good for you.
- Recognize what's controllable. Depression sometimes occurs because life gets out of control. We need to recognize and accept there are going to be things in our life that are out of our control. The weather, for example. Traffic jams. Dropped cellphone calls. True, we can move to where the weather suits us better, never drive, and give up our cellphones. Or we can appreciate these and similar things are simply parts of life, not personal attacks, and they are out of our control. Put effort into what you know you can affect. Control what's controllable and the rest will drop away.
- Schedule "me" time. It may be only a few minutes a day and making time for yourself is critical to overcoming depression. It's simple: if you don't make time for yourself nobody else will. Savor a cup of coffee, listen to one piece of music, watch the wind in the trees. Me time.
- Do what you're good at, slowly. Is there something you know and others know you're particularly good at? Doesn't matter what it is, anything will do. Folding t-shirts, for example, and I'm serious. Something "mundane" works fine. Whatever it is, do it, slowly. Turn folding t-shirts into a Zen experience. It can be very relaxing and relaxation can defeat depression in no time.
- Do something completely different. People understand the term "mental health day", as in taking personal time for no specific reason. Not physical sickness, not an appointment, not

family issues per se, just time away to catch your breath. Take a day off and do something completely different. Walk on a nature trail, visit a museum, take in a lecture, plant a flower, go to a petting zoo, take a round trip to nowhere.

Remember, be good to yourself first.

Birth Control's Long History

I've written before about how diverse my research is. Today's research came up with an indication that women were exercising their reproductive rights some 35,000 years ago.

Think about that (I know I did). We're talking about women in small social groups, family bands, and some 23,000 years before the first known city (Damascus) even came to be.

Hunter-gatherer groups. These women were exercising birth control 26,000 years before agriculture became agriculture.

I'm simply amazed by this.

So how do we know this? Well, the truth is we don't know this for an absolute fact. This falls into the category of "This is our best guess at present based on all the evidence we were able to find". Still, it's an impressive piece of work and it all hinges on how one interprets the image at the end of this chapter:

The image is of an art object found in a cave in Germany in 1979 and is dated to about 35,000 years ago. It's small enough to fit into a pocket.

Ancient iPhone App?

The object can be thought of as an ancient tool — ne' application or app — that allowed women to calculate when their group, tribe, family would be following migratory herds, moving to avoid inclement weather, ... in short calculating when the worst time for birthing would be, hence when to avoid pregnancies that would result in such births.

It worked because it's a mini-map of what the Orion constellation would have looked like some 35,000 years ago from one ancient camp site in what is now Germany. When the stars matched the map — something that only happened for roughly three months of the year — then don't get pregnant.

No idea how they handled roll over minutes and family plans back then, but still ...

Whoa!

Avoiding Self-Destructive Behaviors

The first thing you need to know is that the best way to avoid self-destructive behaviors — those things you do which you don't mean to do that sabotage your work, your partnerships, your life. That's why such behaviors are also often called self-sabotaging and self-defeating behaviors — is to not have them.

That's kind of like "Just say 'No' to drugs," isn't it? Don't want to sabotage yourself? Then don't.

The good news is that just about everybody on the planet has some self-defeating behaviors. Self-defeating behaviors — in their more useful form — are known as our *protective instincts*. Protective instincts are those things that stop us from walking off cliffs, intentionally touching live high tension power lines, things like that. Protective instincts stop us from doing things that might hurt us.

Very useful, don't you think?

Then how did something so very useful become something so … unuseful? Basically self -destructive, -defeating and -sabotaging behaviors are given to us (that's right. They're given to us) in childhood. We hear our mothers say things to our fathers, our fathers to our mothers, a much older and probably care-giving sibling to someone else. We see something done that should not have been done or seen. We believe we did a good thing, something to be proud of, and are punished for it.

Any and all of these things (and many others) occur repeatedly and when we're too young to understand them, to separate the people from the acts or the words, we get wounded in ways too penetrating and permanent to recognize.

The wounding is psycho-emotional, the most difficult to heal. The body, luckily, doesn't remember pain. When the body is wounded it sends a message to the brain, "That hurt! Don't do it again", but it doesn't remember the pain itself. That's the brain's job, to remember to help us avoid.

Which is what happens when we're older, supposedly wiser, going after a job, a promotion, a client, a lover, a friend

Then, suddenly poof, for reasons hidden away, not recognized because we as adults can't access the childhood memories that caused these kinds of trauma (without help and training, anyway), the memories and pains associated with them reveal themselves in behaviors that cause us to put on the brakes, to stop the win, to avoid doing whatever it is we're doing, to defeat, sabotage, and destroy our best efforts by turning them into worst efforts.

Triggering Events

Any behavior is a response to an internal or external event. More accurately, all behaviors are external manifestations of internal responses to internal or external events (what are called BMIRs - Behavioral Manifestation of Internal Response). We drive our cars, cook our dinners, hug others, and push still others away because our lifelong memories dictate how we respond to events happening around us now.

The same is true for self-defeating, destructive, etc., behaviors. We respond in the moment with a life time of experience. What we need to do is recognize what events trigger which behaviors.

An Example

A small company CEO always seemed to take vacations whenever a client was ready to sign, a product was about to be released, a milestone was about to be achieved, … , whenever anything critical to company progress was going to happen, the CEO … well … vanished. Couldn't be reached by phone, by email, knocks on the door or requests to family and friends.

Company success was unobtainable because the individual leading the company psycho-emotionally refused to lead when the need for leadership was at its peak.

And it was all traceable to a mother who never honored a father's best efforts, demonstrated that lack of honoring in front of her children, and, as this individual grew, refused to honor this individual's best efforts as well.

When the repeated message is that no best effort is worthy, the desire to put forth a best effort fades — after all, it won't be honored — so while the conscious mind wants us to achieve, the lifetime of experience instructs us to avoid.

Changing Responses

Knowing your personal history of self -destructive, -defeating, -sabotaging, … behaviors is part of the solution and is best done with professional help. After that knowledge comes learning to recognize what events trigger those behaviors. This takes a willingness to become self-aware that in itself can be a difficult and painful journey (although an incredibly worthwhile one (in my opinion) for those so willing).

It is while on this last journey that we learn to control our behaviors, to respond to events as we wish to rather than how we used to, to change what we were to what we can be.

It is up to us as individuals to decide.

Addendum

The person who taught me these things has long passed and I'm writing this post to pass on that learning to a friend, the CEO mentioned above, and including another lesson from this same master: My journey is my goal, my path is my prize.

Knowing, learning and changing is what life is all about. No matter where your path takes you, rejoice in it. No matter what your journey entails, relish it.

Going It Alone

There is an oddity about humans as a social species that I think about from time to time: more often women go it alone — live solo — in our society than men do.

There are reasons for this. People who've heard my presentations on male and female buying behaviors know that women are great strategic investors, men are better tactically.

This difference in our neural patterns makes itself known in lots of ways. One way is that women (not in all cases, just more often than not) are monogamous, men the reverse (and again, not in all cases, simply more often than not. Our current monogamously directed culture has more to do with economics than biology).

Women, because they think in the long term without even knowing they're thinking in the long term, will go it alone when no suitable long term investment (a good life-partner prospect) presents itself. Men, often without thinking of this specifically, are willing to take the immediate risk of a possibly unsatisfying relationship because they don't really think of the implications of that risk down the road.

I often joke about how this plays out in courting. Women want to meet the family. They may not know why and non-consciously they want to know if the seed has fallen far from the tree, so to speak. They will observe the family of origin and put that into their calculations for long term potential and expectations.

Men will agree to meet the family because it's expected. They will observe non-consciously to determine their hierarchy in the potentially extended clan.

Example: I dated one girl and was getting close to thinking long term with her. Prior to posing the question, I traveled to meet her family. Her father and two brothers invited me into the basement to play a game of pool. I won. Because I was focusing on my shots, I didn't notice that with each pocketed ball the three males around me grew colder and colder.

While I was not attempting to establish my hierarchy, I violated theirs. My strong female side (a female friend once told her other female friends "You don't have to worry about Joseph. He's not really a guy." I'm recognized as both a Contrary and Sacred Clown in cultures that have those concepts) warned me quite clearly that this was not a family I wanted to be involved with.

Behaviors should not be confused with life decisions here. Women may date, etc., just as much if not more than men do.

But it's the life-long decisions that I'm writing about here. I remember, when I was a child and long before I knew the story of Hansel and Gretel, often going to visit an (to me at the time, I was less than three years old) old, old woman who lived deep in a wood near my home.

Okay, it seemed deep in a wood to me. Many years later the childhood myth was given reality and I'll get to that later.

Several children would go and visit her. She always had cookies, candy, milk, apples. And she would read to us and tell us stories of places she'd been.

The older children — those who no longer visited her — told us she was a witch. What else could she be? An old woman who lived alone in a small house deep in a woods?

Eventually my family moved and many years later I asked my older sisters if they knew about the old woman who lived alone in the woods. My mother overheard the question and laughed.

The old woman was — when I visited her — in her mid-fifties — my age now. She had been a school teacher who had traveled the world with her husband, a high-ranking soldier who served at embassies across the globe. Her two sons she lost in the Korean War years earlier and now, living on both hers and her husband's pensions, she lived on the other side of the hill, one side of which was occupied by my family, the other side by other families. Her home was simply closest to the edge of the trees that crested the hill. Total distance from my backdoor to hers?

About one-hundred-and-fifty feet.

How did she get to be known as a witch?

"Because of the stories, I guess," my mother explained. "She was an unofficial baby-sitter for your aunts and me. We knew when you and your cousins were heading in her direction and knew you'd be safe with her. We'd go see her for tea sometimes. The places she'd been. Her stories were like magic. They took you there."

And as my mother's eyes misted over I remembered hearing my aunts and mother talk more than once, in the presence of us kids and without realizing how closely we listened and heard, about "the magic in her stories."

Hence a witch was born.

But she never remarried? I asked.

"She never wanted to. She told me once that one man was all she needed, that he had been enough, and the memories of him would last her forever."

Should we ever meet, dear reader, I hope I can tell you stories of myth, magic and places so vivid and rich that my words propel you to distant lands and times, and that when you leave me, you think me a witch or wizard, and I will be glad.

Be Honest with Yourself, Be Honest with Others, Be at Peace

What does one do when someone tells you, "I don't have a problem lying to people."

It's kind of like that old logic problem: you go to the Land of the Liars where everybody tells falsehoods. The first person you meet makes two statements:
1. The next statement I make will be a lie.
2. The last statement I made was a lie.

I've met only a few people who actually told me "I don't have a problem lying to people" however I'm well aware that the attitude exists regardless of its being stated as such. And I'll admit such attitudes pose a challenge to me because, as one friend confided to me, "Your commitment to the truth outweighs your commitment to people's feelings — particularly when dealing with idiots or assholes — but it's a close race."

My first and greatest suggestion when dealing with such individuals is to separate yourself from them. Their reputations will eventually become blackened and so will yours (by association if nothing else).

I also realize there are a variety of social reasons that would preclude one from distancing oneself from such individuals.

Let me first offer ways to recognize habitual or professional liars, then some ways to protect yourself from their ways.

Recognition Methods

Fortunately, we're dealing with people who have a very well defined and detailed set of characteristics, they are pathologic or compulsive ("habitual" and "chronic" fall into this category) liars and are not sociopaths. Do you know someone who:

- Seeks approval from others?
- Won't take a firm stand on any topic?
- Changes jobs often?
- Has family problems?
- Won't disagree except on trivial matters?
- Won't admit to mistakes and errors?
- Tends to think in absolutes (all/nothing, black/white, yes/no)?
- Doesn't live up to their promises, regardless of how insignificant?

The list can go on quite a ways and what's above is sufficient. Remember, one or two or even three do not a pathologic or compulsive liar make and the more you can check off the more likely the individual will tell a lie over the truth whenever it suits their purpose.

That last part is the important part, " … whenever it suits their purpose." The truth or lack thereof is, to them, a tool to be used to achieving a goal.

My suggestion is to be wary of them.

Protecting Yourself

The best method for protecting yourself from their lying ways is two-fold. First, the title of this post, "Be Honest with Yourself, Be Honest with Others, Be at Peace". You need this first part to keep your wits about you to do the second: document all your conversations, interactions, keep an email thread, a chat log, whatever, of each and every encounter with such individuals. In business, this is called due diligence. In life it's called "being wise as serpents and harmless as doves".

I really need to emphasize that "Be Honest with Yourself, Be Honest with Others, Be at Peace" part. Few things can thwart the habitual fabricator more than honesty and the place to start being honest is with yourself. Should someone be reading this who recognizes themselves as a compulsive or pathologic liar, this is where you start your path towards truth (should that be of interest to you). The more you can be honest with yourself about anything and everything the more you'll be able to speak honestly to others.

Closely tied to "Be Honest with Yourself, Be Honest with Others" is the third beat, "Be at Peace". Your truth and honesty can create a cloud of calm in any storm, so go for it.

And you'll find that being honest with yourself, honest with others, and at peace allows you to objectively and subjectively document encounters with those who are less able truthtellers than you are. You can find some basic suggestions for this in the opening paragraphs of The Unfulfilled Promise of Online Analytics, Part 3 - Determining the Human Cost (up to "All Manner of People Tell Me All Manner of Things"). (see link)

This Is On My Mind Because ...

By the time this post goes live my company, NextStage Evolution (*see Appendix: Definitions for more context -ed.*), will have released its BSMeter tool, created at the request of a client and now going public, the tool determines whether or not someone is imagining or creating information rather than observing or recalling information.

Technically, someone who tells you of the wonderful future you'll have together is using the same brain areas as someone who tells you they responded to a client when they didn't. Both are imagining or creating information.

Technically, I'd call the latter a liar, the former ... well ... that's a fabrication most can easily recognize and are happy to live with.

Predicting Your Own Future

There is a technique I occasionally perform with people in crisis. It basically lets me know how convinced they are regarding their ability to get out of crisis, what it will take to get them out of crisis, what they believe got them into crisis, obstacles, … it's a neat tool that, fortunately, I won't demonstrate in this section.

What I will demonstrate, though, is a recent use of it (and keeping everything anonymous, of course). An early 30's male I know was experiencing family problems. He and his wife hadn't been husband and wife (ahem) in better than a year, he often mentioned wanting to escape — that was the term he used, escape — from his wife and child, he was failing in business due to emotional problems.

This was not a happy camper.

So I asked permission to have him travel to his future. He could only report what he saw, he couldn't change anything he saw.

In a few short leaps he was witnessing his son's college graduation. He could tell he was proud, felt himself beaming, waved at his son and his son waved back.

"Could you look around you and tell me what you see? Who's there?" He did. His wife was nowhere to be found. "Do you recognize any of the other people there?" There were a few from his side of the family there. Lots of other people he didn't know.

"I'd like you to come back a few years and look around you. Tell me what you see. Is it warm or cold? Do you know where you are?"

We repeated this until he was back sitting in his living room.

What we learned from this exercise was when he believed he and his wife would separate and why (finances, mainly, although family issues and a lack of mutual trust played a role as well), who would go where and do what, so on and so forth.

The above is just a description of this type of exercise. It turns out most people are remarkably adept at predicting their own futures. Not necessarily places and events, per se, but relationships, jobs, roles in society, finances, things like that.

Provided they are truthful with themselves (as mentioned in Be Honest With Yourself, Be Honest With Others, Be At Peace).

So the next time you feel yourself unsure of where you're going in life, or that you're in crisis or just wondering how things will turn out for you.

Close your eyes … listen carefully … breathe …

The Liz Effect

> *It is precisely because a child's feelings are so strong that they cannot be repressed without serious consequences. The stronger a prisoner is, the thicker the prison walls have to be, which impede or completely prevent later emotional growth. - Alice Miller,* The Drama of the Gifted Child

I've written about The Joseph Effect - people's desire to behave in a way conducive to NextStage's Principles (see Appendix: Principles), who ask themselves "What would Joseph do?" when faced with certain situations - elsewhere (see Understanding and Using NextStage's Level 1 Sentiment Analysis Tool and "It's too accurate" (more undocumented uses of NextStage's Evolution Technology) via the links at the end of the book).

It got me to thinking about people whose examples have affected me one way or another and the lessons I learned along the way. The good effects are pretty much demonstrated by NextStage's Principles. But I believe in measuring the good with the not so good, so exploring the not so good is often a way to manifest good where it otherwise might not have existed.

In this case, lessons learned from a long-ex girlfriend, Liz, hence The Liz Effect. Liz was a recognizably attractive woman subjected to the whims of an amazingly insecure inner-child's psyche. In the limited time I spent with her I realized her incredible insecurities stemmed from her parents' unequal marriage: an incredibly insecure yet wonderfully capable father yoked to an extremely intelligent, visually stunning mother who sacrificed a promising career because, coming home from work one day, she found her home stripped, her children missing and a note on the door, "Decided to become a plumber, moved everything to dad's cottage, will keep dinner warm for you."

To suggest that her parents' relationship failed - they stopped living together while living in the same house - is to equate an R10 earthquake to the slitherings of an earthworm.

Liz was still a little girl when this happened and as often happens when families suffer abrupt and stunning changes in pattern, the psychic and emotional wounds healed by developing methods of protecting that little girl for the rest of Liz's life.

People rarely psycho-emotionally mature after such trauma and, unlike scars to the body, scars to the mind are never easy to see let alone recognize. These people can function in society only until environmental stressors cause them to protect that child.

In Liz's case, the protective layer was to make sure nothing got emotionally close enough to cause the "father" she carried in her child's mind to take flight. This protective layer was learned by watching her parents' interactions and reactions of her parents the rest of her life - belittling, bigoted, antagonistic and hateful to anything that challenged their self-imposed status quo. Anybody she didn't know was either stupid or a fool until proven otherwise (and once decided, no one including she could prove otherwise). Anybody who didn't agree with her was both stupid and a fool regardless if she knew them or not. She insulted people she knew when they weren't around and, if bested in a discussion, often took out her frustration on inanimate objects (she broke things. Usually the things of those who bested her. If they weren't available, anybody else's things would do. Even when they weren't involved in the discussion to begin with. I don't remember her ever breaking her things).

Liz once told me to decide between her and my dog (at the time a beautiful Newfoundland named Maschaak ("Messenger of God")).

Liz's roommate was moving out. Liz couldn't afford the rent on her own. She insisted I move in even though my place had plenty of room. But her place didn't allow pets. So I suggested we compromise and find a place she liked that did allow pets.

No, wrong, that's not what she wanted me to do. So I said I'd stay where I was, with Maschaak, and she could stay with us until she found a place.

Again, idiot moi, I simply wasn't paying attention. How I couldn't understand the simplicity of the situation demonstrated just what a stupid fool I was.

And she told me what a stupid fool I was in these terms, "You better figure out what's important to you, mister. That dog will be gone in a few years and I'll be around the rest of your life. Choose that dog over me and you're an even bigger fool than I thought you were."

Maschaak lived another ten years and his ashes are on my bookshelf. He liked being with me in my office so I keep him here still, and when I reach for a math or philosophy text I still pet him and like to think I'm rubbing him behind his ears.

Liz didn't last the rest of that summer.

And the language when I told her my decision …

Noting The Liz Effect in Your Life

Life is full of decisions and whether they'll be easy or hard is based on too many factors to count here.

But a way to make a hard decision easier to deal with is to share it with someone who makes no demands on the outcome, who listens, who incurs no obligations for a yay or nay, who accepts your choice as yours even if they know it wouldn't work for them and lastly, who'll be with you — not necessarily to defend you, more necessarily to bandage any wounds that might occur should your decision not be the best — no matter which way the decision or its outcome goes.

Cherish those people when you meet them. Keep them close.

People who demand you make a decision only do so because they want you to decide a certain way (in their favor, usually. If someone wants you to decide against them walk away slowly, carefully, and don't turn your back on them when you do).

The decision isn't important, it's their desire to control your decision, hence you, and once you give up control of your own decisions finding your way back is very, very difficult. Demanding you make a decision they want you to make is an exercise in control, nothing else and nothing less.

Keep yourself in control of yourself. You'll have less to worry about.

Addendum

I happened to bump into Liz years later. Maschaak was sitting beside me in my pickup, we were heading up to Quebec through New Hampshire and Maine and the roads led us through her town (thoroughly convinced her beauty, intellect, and charm would take her around the world, she never left the town where her granddad's cottage was and where her parents are buried).

And there she was, walking down the side of the road, still intent, still highly focused, still protecting that inner-child from anything anyone could ask of it.

I pulled up beside her, rolled down the window and asked how she'd been and if she needed a ride.

"Still have that fucking dog, I see."

I laughed. I had no choice. I wished her well and continued on my way. It was another three-plus hours to the Canadian border and I sobbed through most of them while Maaschak licked my face.

There are no stronger, no longer lasting prisons than the ones we construct for ourselves. There are no jailors more aware of our every attempted escape, more willing to reinforce our incarceration, than we ourselves.

If you're reading this and you sometimes sense those walls or are experiencing The Liz Effect in your life, here's your chance.

Breakout!

Did You See What He Was Wearing?

I share a little story in *Reading Virtual Minds Volume 1: Science and History* (see link at the end of the book) about how a woman, a complete stranger to me, helped me pick out a pair of pants while I was shopping. Lots of readers contact me about that story. One of the reasons for the story is that both the woman and I were middle-aged. Another, even more significant reason the incident described could take place is because I was purchasing casual pants. Nothing flashy, nothing extravagant, nothing intended to catch people's eyes.

Well, that last part isn't exactly true. It has more to do with knowing how to catch specific eyes. I've been doing some research on how to "catch someone's eye" and there's an interesting little tidbit that applies to males regardless of age and culture. What's also interesting is that it applies to whatever the male is purchasing or owns. It goes like this:
- Take a male of any age. That male is in a comfortable relationship with a mature woman if they are conservative in dress, style, language, accents, accoutrements, self-identification

and personality extensions. What does "conservative" mean? Darker colors, primarily in western culture, whites, blacks or grays in Asia. Thin stripes on shirts, slacks, suits, ties. When you look at them you'll probably come away recognizing self-assuredness, personal power, personal awareness, assertiveness without aggressiveness, confidence, ... This will show up in cars, brands they are drawn to, things like that (that's self-identification and personality extensions).

- Take a male of any age. That male is in an uncomfortable relationship with a mature woman if they are loud in dress, style, language, accents, ... basically more flash and brighter colors. Most times you'll come away with a sense of aggressiveness (not assertiveness).

And, of course, it's switched if the male of any age is in a comfortable relationship with a younger woman - look for Bling! Is the relationship with the younger woman on the skids? Look for conservative personal styling.

What's interesting about this is that it's a pure male behavior. Get one-hundred younger women in a room and ask, "Given the same guy, do you go for bling or no bling?" and you'll get a fairly even split depending on things like culture, location, language and so on. Same for mature women.

The take away for guys on this one is pretty much the one that will open a woman's heart each and every time — be yourself. Did you always go for the bling? Don't stop now. It's your personal style, your mark, your brand, and you'll feel awkward without it. Forget what your friends have told you, women don't pity an awkward suitor. In ethology studies, awkwardness would be a sign of reproductive unfitness and humans — males and females — are still wired to pay attention to those rules.

Likewise, if your personal style is towards the conservative side, go with it. Regardless of whose eye you want to catch, you'll catch the eye of someone who'll care about you as you and not some idea of you that ain't really true.

Fear of Rejection

I was contacted by someone whose personal life is interfering with their public life.

First, in a Facebook, LinkedIn, YouTube, Twitter world, I detect some kind of oxymoron in the thought that public and private lives are still separate.

Second, throughout all history it has been impossible for most people — barring sociopaths — to keep their private life and public life separate. I've known some people who are remarkably adept at compartmentalizing things and this doesn't mean they're keeping things separate, only that they're letting specific things through.

The reason it's impossible to keep different aspects of our lives separate is because all aspects of our lives are "powered" by our core psychologies and beliefs. Someone who's a joy on the job and a terror at home is simply bringing their work frustrations home and letting them out there. The reason people act out at home (private life) more than at work (public life) is because the relative safety of the home allows for more of the core to manifest itself.

Usually.

But this chapter is about *Fear of Rejection*, so let's get to it ... This individual's family-of-origin (the core family group that raised you) didn't support open emotionality (Note to parents: unless children learn how to express their emotions openly they'll never learn when it's not safe to do so). This lack of support planted a seed of emotional confusion and frustration.

Such seeds usually sprout polarity type demonstrations. The individual either grows cold (never having learned how to demonstrate emotions healthily the safest thing for them to do is shut theirs down when presented with yours) or demonstrates their emotions too easily and often (never having learned how to demonstrate emotions healthily they've never learned boundaries and limits to their own emotional displays). At the best of times there's a median ground where the individual doesn't grow completely cold with certain individuals or learns with whom it is safe to be emotional.

In this case, that seed was watered when a poor partner choice paired them with someone who could not honor commitments and philandered. Often.

And what sprouted is a fear of rejection.

As noted above, this fear wasn't compartmentalized to one aspect of life. What happened in their private life manifested in their public life. Seeking a new job, they decided the potential employer was not interested (and worse, if you know how these phobias make themselves known).

So they contacted me for some advice, and I share that advice with all those possibly facing similar fears.

Advice to the fearful

Your partner (I assume now an ex-partner)'s philandering was an indication of their psyche, not yours. You've decided their actions were due to some lack or inability on your part hence you've "developed a fear of rejection".

"Fear of rejection" isn't something that happens overnight.

Nobody wakes up one morning, stretches, throws back the covers, looks smilingly into the sun and declares, "Yes, from this day forward I shall fear rejection!" This response - because that's what it is, it's a response to your environment - was something taught to you and learned over time. Because it was taught and learned, because it's not part of how you're designed to work, it can be unlearned, untaught, and more useful responses can take its place.

By the way, you were designed to be wonderful. Just like everybody else. If you're not wonderful right now, it's someone else's responsibility. Your parents, your partners, your co-workers, your supervisors, your friends, ...

But (*BUT!!!*) if you're reading this right now, you are being invited to take responsibility *from them* - they're obviously not good stewards of you - and put it where it belongs, *in you*.

Scary, I know, that "taking responsibility for yourself" part. We are what we've put our greatest efforts into creating and it took us our whole lives to become the way we are. It's tough to re-do a work of art so far along in its creation and that's okay, we're designed to be able to do it. It's part of that evolutionary process that's in our DNA.

I would offer that you've created a tool for dealing with certain types of information. Now you must decide if the tool you've developed — a fear of rejection — is the best tool for dealing with the "no information coming in" type of information, the "negative" information, and other certain types of information. Dealing with negative information - the type of information we'd rather not have - is pretty easy. First determine if it's valid information. It is? Then change the reason for the negative information (maybe it's time to change a job because of a harsh boss, change a partner because they don't care about you, change your brand of soap or laundry detergent, ...). It isn't valid? Ignore it and its source.

Right. Now let's deal with the "no information coming in" type of information. Often when people are waiting for a response from someone or something and they get no response whatsoever, they imagine the worst. In relationships (professional and personal) this becomes fear of rejection.

So first recognize you're using the fear of rejection tool to deal with "no information coming in".

Next, recognize that information is coming in, simply not information you have a good tool for. The information is "no information" because (without boring you with jargon) an information "vacuum" can not exist. The vacuum is being filled with information from your past experiences, and specifically your "fear of rejection" experiences.

As with your partner, so with this potential employer: whatever their response, they're making a statement about themselves, not about you. Your life-partner's philandering was a statement of their limits, their lack, and how they sought to fill them. It was a demonstration of their lack of tools and had nothing to do with you.

Really, truly, it is so. Believe it.

There's a tool I use, not specific to "fear of rejection" although I'm betting it would work quite well because it is a "fill the vacuum with correct information" tool. I contact people and ask them, "Have you made a decision yet?"

I know, you're shocked that I would be direct and to the point, yes?

This tool is built on another tool, an Eliadean tool, known as "choice is better than no choice". I believe knowing is better than not knowing, hence my desire to know as a fact that I'm "rejected" is stronger than my desire to remain ignorant of such a fact because knowing facts allows me choices. Not knowing limits my choices.

Knowing something is a fact allows me to make decisions and choices based on that piece of information. Not knowing makes me a victim of my ignorance, traps me in a well of uncertainty, and forces me to stop functioning until I learn what fact applies.

More to the case here, it causes me to live a life of fear rather than a life of joy, bliss, happiness, love, … And I do know that how I choose to live my life directly affects all those around me. Living a life of fear will cause me to demonstrate fear-based behaviors to everyone I'm in contact with, especially those I love. If I interact daily with children? They will learn the "fear of rejection" lesson and the more I interact with them the better they will learn it.

So for me I'll chose a life of bliss, joy, happiness and love because I'd rather people drink those things from my cup than any others.

Take to the Road

How do you determine if someone is more or less likely to produce healthy children? Is there one, single factor that tends to outweigh all others? Strangely enough, there is. And if someone had mentioned what it is to me offhandedly I would be skeptical. Truthfully and with the research in front of me, I'm still a little skeptical. Until I think about it. What we're talking about is reproductive fitness and while I never would have said "A key to having healthy offspring is to travel more" I can't deny the findings.

It's pretty simple in lots of ways. The more traveled someone is, the more likely they are to have encountered a wide variety of pathogens (diseases). The more pathogens someone has encountered and survived - that's a critical part, surviving the diseases - the more likely they are to pass these survival genes on to their progeny. And it's not enough to survive. You can't survive at the loss of a limb or with some obvious deformation.

I know, we live in a muchly enlightened society and physical abnormalities no longer matter to us. Right … uh-huh … yeah. If such were the case we wouldn't need to legislate anti-discrimination based on race, creed, color, ethnicity, age, health, … we wouldn't need to write laws telling insurance companies what to do with pre-existing conditions, we wouldn't need to write hiring laws dictating equal employment opportunities, … Because all those things we're legislating for or against? Those were things that helped us survive - there's "survive" again - as a family, as a group, as a tribe, as a town, as a culture, as a nation, … for ever so long. As a group they are known as "fear of the 'other'"

Guarding against and fearing those who were different from us kept us alive when we went from the trees to the pampas to the village to the nation. Fear of the Other is very much a part of our modern, enlightened social psychology.

What to do, what to do, what to do? We create laws to defeat our instincts and learnings of many thousands if not a few million years of evolutionary history. I know the need for these laws is a legacy of my parents' generation and all those who came before them. I also know prejudices, bigotry, hatred, etc., are, like genes, passed on from parents to children.

The diseases of prejudice, bigotry, hatred, etc., still exist. We see them as epidemics in places like Afghanistan, Darfur, India, Iraq, Israel, Mexico, Palestine, Pakistan, Somalia, Sudan, … We see them as virus outbreaks in terrorist and similar attacks around the globe. Few of the deadliest conflicts in the world today are completely economic in nature. Few people are fighting over water holes or mineral rights. Most of the deadliest conflicts are because the person on the other end of the gun is wearing different clothes, has different beliefs, talks different, looks different, … we are still tribes. Enlightened tribes, perhaps, and we're still tribal in nature.

I have no idea how long these diseases will survive. I suspect — again based on laws of evolutionary biology, epidemiology, cultural anthropology, sociology, … - they will always be with us. It is horrible and true that these diseases help those who survive them (again, in both mind and limb) to pass on more survival related genes to their offspring than those who don't survive them. It is scary how closely social diseases' pathologies mimic biologic diseases' pathologies.

But the funny thing is … While being well traveled and returning healthy and whole is an indicator of reproductive fitness from an evolutionary biology perspective, it increasingly makes sense in enlightening the world, as well. People who are well traveled tend to be more tolerant of others, more accepting of differences, more understanding of inexperience, more respectful of others' opinions and more comfortable with themselves hence more comfortable with others. Now those are great things to pass on to your children, me thinks. Great genes and a great attitude to an increasingly diverse culture?

So, if you want healthy, happy children, take to the road.

A 3AM Phone Call

The phone rang at 3AM and even as I rose from slumber, I knew a casual conversation would not ensue. Phone calls at odd hours are indicative of great emotions, usually. So it was with this one. Someone was calling because they were in emotional crisis. They called me because they knew me — sort of — and had read what I'd written about being overwhelmed and felt I was someone they could reach out to.

First, give them credit that they knew the problem was a massive feeling of inability, of being unable to do, act, or perform to expectations.

Second, give them credit that they reached out for help. Feeling overwhelmed is often a prelude to depression so good for them, they caught things in time.

With any such challenge, having these two elements means you're better than 90% of the way to a solution, so congratulations to you. What I offer here is a path to going the other ten percent. Remember, I'm not a professional therapist and you should seek out a professional therapist if feeling overwhelmed habitually plagues you. I asked the individual what was overwhelming them. "Work."

Were there too many projects? Was management expecting too much? "No, I don't think so."

Then I didn't understand how they were becoming overwhelmed. "It's me. I always feel I need to get things done now. People ask me to do something and if I can't get what they asked for to them immediately then I've failed and they won't want me anymore, they won't love me anymore."

Did you notice what happened there?

The individual started talking about work and in one sentence demonstrated that external forces — work, management, co-workers — probably had nothing to do with this feeling. They used the word "now" and the phrase " … they won't want me anymore, they won't love me anymore."

I won't go into agonizing details here and simply offer that "now" as used here is what's called a mythic concept, meaning its use is probably coming from childhood memories. Similarly, " … they won't want me anymore, they won't love me anymore." used so closely together, the latter explaining the former, is not indicative of an adult, work place psychology.

Put the two together and I wondered if we were dealing with some childhood issues.

Digging into Someone's Past - ArchaeoPsychology

I asked this individual to tell me more about having to get things done "now". Was it really important to get things done "now"? Was there anything that could wait until "later"?

It took about half an hour, much of it spent in silence as the individual worked for an answer. Again, without going into details, there were many emotional statements made. I listened and let this person speak, to unload, to share.

Finally, an unemotional statement, a completely neutrally toned statement, spoken casually as if offered in lunch table conversation about the weather, "I remember when I was about five or six years old, my father was working downstairs and it was late at night, maybe nine or ten o'clock. My sisters and I were getting ready for bed and our father called for us to help him. We all ran because you never kept dad waiting. I was only in my skivvies, I had nothing else on. Dad spanked me hard on the bottom and yelled at me that I wasn't ready, I wasn't dressed, and I wasn't any good to him unless I was ready to get to work."

And I paused. No more came. I counted my own breaths and asked, "Any more memories like that?"

There were no more memories like that. I asked a few different ways to make sure. In answer, this individual said with timidity, "I realized then that I always had to be ready to work, to get things done, or dad wouldn't love me. I'd get a beating if I couldn't do what he wanted when he wanted it done."

And I said, "What a horrible way to go through life."

Hyperboles from Childhood

First, usually no single such childhood message gains such psychological power over adulthood unless it's reinforced fairly often during childhood. Such was the case here. This individual's father — I'm guessing he had his own issues and wasn't dealing with them very well — often would decide to perform some household maintenance when it was least likely others would be able to help him — an indication of the issues he was dealing with, perhaps — then go into a rage when the help that arrived was less than required — his own hyperbolic from his own childhood.

Adults who often have extreme reactions to everyday events, reactions that are not based on physiologic challenges, tend to be responding from childhood.

Let me give you an example. Have you ever witnessed a child respond to a situation very maturely? Far more maturely than their years would permit? Chances are their precocity is a mimicry of an adult care-giver's response to a similar situation. The child, wanting to be loved and learning how to navigate a world greatly populated by big people (adults), does what the adult does in hopes of being loved, fitting in, being accepted and cared for.

This mimicry done often enough and rewarded with hugs, kisses, pats on the head, treats, is reinforced and becomes adult behaviors. The child who's willing to work long and hard, who learns that by working long and hard beside their parents, is rewarded by their parents, their extended family, the community at large and eventually in the adult world and in business for being a good worker.

Now imagine that precocious response in the negative, as a defense against not being loved, not being accepted, not fitting in, being abandoned, given the stick instead of the carrot.

As with the above, done often enough and that childhood conditioning becomes adulthood crippling.

Children grow up to become hyperboles - as when we use an extreme example to focus attention on a single detail, like talking in hyperboles - of their parents. Both the good and the bad.

Let me give you an example. Let's say three or so generations ago your great-great-great-great grandmother sat at her kitchen table with her children peeling apples from a bushel basket and chatting about the upcoming town social. She reaches into the basket and snaps her hand back suddenly. A spider crawls over the back of her hand and she goes, "Oh!" because she's startled. She slaps the spider, killing it, then wipes the remains on her apron.

Her children see their mother startled and suddenly excited. Something similar happens a few more times, but only when your great-great-great grandfather is around. Now an adult, he's working in his home while his children watch and a spider webs its way down in front of him. He pulls back, knocks it away, then rubs his hand frantically to get any web residue off. He keeps checking around to make sure the spider's not around. Something similar happens a few more times but only when your great-great aunt is around.

Now she's working in her garden with her children. A spider

scurries across the ground in front of her. She leaps up, her face white, her feet dancing a mad tattoo and her skirts held high, almost indecently high, as she attempt to kill the spider and keeps dancing until the spider is long dead and the ground flattened with her efforts, and all while her children watch.

And as before, her children watch. This story repeats through generations, each time a child or children hyperbolizing their parent's reaction, until you're sitting in your modern home watching your big screen TV and see a innocuous spider crawling on the wall beside it and have a full blown panic attack because you've inherited an irrational fear of spiders.

Talk about even unto the seventh generation!

Some people spend most of their adult lives taming these hyperboles from childhood and others - such as this individual's father, me thinks - merely continue to live them out and go deeper into their own private hell.

Taming the Shrew

The suggestion I made was simple enough and seems to be working. It's probably working because it's simple. Also because it makes use of the "Every strength is a weakness, every weakness is a strength" teaching.

Would it be possible to break up each work task — indeed, any task, work or otherwise — into a bunch of minor tasks? If the task was writing a report, then the minor tasks were sitting at the computer, starting up the word processor, choosing a report template, ... ?

"Of course. But what good is that?"

Could we then assign each task — note that I no longer defined each task as "minor" — to its own private "now"? Instead of all the tasks — again, nothing "minor" here — occurring in a single "now", could each task have its own "now" so that there was one and only one task that needed to be accomplished in each "now"?

There was about two minutes of silence. A very long time as we closed into 4AM. Finally, a quiet "Yes."

The long silence and quiet response indicated this individual was changing how they thought — how they worked — at a very deep psychological level.

Tell me about the projects you have going on at work. Think of them as if they were a picture. Tell me what you see. "There're long lines of events, of separate nows, streaming out and away from me. Each line of events is a separate project."

They paused. I guessed they were working on something else, something more, and gave them time. Then, "I can walk from one stream to the other and back. I don't have to get everything done at once anymore. I can wait while something is finishing up over here and go do something over there and then come back. That always used to bother me, having to wait for something to get done before being able to finish what I was working on."

And I knew we were complete

The true success of such things is when the individual both implements and augments the suggestion. Implementing my suggestion left it still my suggestion. Augmenting it so that it also dealt with another, unexpressed issue made it their suggestion, meaning they were now more invested in its success.

Please don't think things that took years to get into you are going to come out in seconds. By the time you recognize them your mind has adapted them to serve many purposes and removing them "in a moment" only means they'll manifest themselves in other ways you were unaware of. The typical example of this is the individual who quits smoking and gains weight. Understand the why of smoking and you'll understand what has to be done to quit without side-effects.

And as always, just my opinion, that.

The Lady on the Table

During some recent travels we stayed at a B&B and spent some time having tea and cookies with the other guests and Innkeepers.

The Innkeeper, a wonderfully brassy woman who's led a varied life, asked if we'd mind if she made her weekly call to some friends in France (we were in Nova Scotia) and we said of course, go ahead, not a problem at all.

She then put her laptop on the coffee table, opened up a video-conference call package, and we heard a familiar "ring-ring" followed by a child's delighted laughter.

The innkeeper made some funny faces and clapped her hands and cried out "Bonjour!".

We heard more childish laughter, tiny hands clapping and a giddily happy shriek of "Mama, Mama, la dame sur la table!"

"I've watched that child grow from belly to birth to that babe on the screen." She turned the laptop so we could all see the family gather an ocean away. Some of us waved. The child and mother so far away waved back.

They spent about ten minutes catching up on life and then the call was over.

"How did you folks meet?" I asked.

The woman and her husband had toured Canada and spent a night at the B&B. When they got home she realized she was pregnant and that their night at this B&B had been the night, so she emailed the innkeeper with the news.

"Wow. Neat."

They made an agreement to stay in touch so the innkeepers could watch the child grow.

We smiled.

"Does the little girl know who you are?" I asked.

Of course she does. What a silly question. "I'm the lady on the table." So named because once a week a laptop is placed on a coffee table in a home somewhere in France and a video chat client is opened and the miles melt into smiles and children's laughter.

Here's to hoping there are only smiles in children's futures.

Unhealthy Comparisons

I recently met a fellow who admitted he's spent better than half his life comparing himself to people, some he knew, others simply public figures.

I never found that a useful exercise so I asked him about it. Was making comparisons pleasurable? Did it make him happy? Basically, what was his gain?

He confided it wasn't always a pleasant exercise for him. There were two types of comparisons he made. One was where he recognized traits or abilities others had that he lacked and set about acquiring those traits or abilities in the belief his life would be better. Such endeavors could be painful but were ultimately beneficial to him and those around him. Psychology recognizes this as benign envy.

The other type came in his "black" times, when he was depressed or inconsolable, and mainly consisted of thinking others had benefits he never had and none of the troubles he did have. This is known as malicious envy in psychological circles.

Here, in one person, the two primary types of "comparing oneself to others" were demonstrated, the former benign and usually beneficial, the latter malicious and usually crippling.

Research on this phenomenon goes back to the mid 1950s and is known as Social Comparison Theory. There are lots of excellent resources on the 'net dealing with overcoming the crippling side of this issue and if you're someone who has this challenge, please search for "comparing oneself to others" and take a look. I didn't know these resources existed until I sat down to write this.

First, I shared with this fellow that I, too, compare myself to others. I've even documented this in Mistaken Identities, Part 3 (see link at the end of the book) and the other posts in that series. There are lots of people whom I meet or learn about and note some qualities they have — more charitable, more loving, more generous, for example — that I want to increase or simply want, period. Often I'll seek them out via email, phone or in person and ask their guidance (I've been doing it since I was a teenager).

But people are the sum of their parts. One of the first things I learned about doing this was I'm sometimes mistaken about them. The qualities I want they don't actually possess. They can demonstrate them but these qualities aren't part of their core, a case of "squeeze an orange and you'll get orange juice". (one of the NextStage Principles, see appendix)

Okay, take a step back. Do I still want that quality I thought they had? Then go for it on my own. My experience is eventually a mentor shows up who can guide me through the learning and acquisition process.

But back to oranges and orange juice for a moment. Learning an individual's public and private personae could be deeply incongruous taught me to observe better, to pay more attention, to isolate the qualities from the individual demonstrating them and model that quality alone.

I asked this fellow if he could do something similar.

Yes.

But people are complex and whole. Single qualities — generosity, for example — usually don't manifest overnight. Most people who easily demonstrate a single quality gain that ability from lots of practice. It's really no different than Michael Jordan at basketball or John Mellencamp writing songs. True, they may have a natural inclination for such things, a gift of genetics, but natural gifts can only go so far and then both the individual, their life, their past and present surroundings all play a role.

Benign envy is working for you, I said, so let's look at malicious envy. You have to make a choice:

- You get to have all the benefits, all the breaks and all the luck that person you're comparing yourself has had.
- But this means you must take on all the detriments, all the brickwalls and all the bad luck that person has had. The person you're comparing yourself to is the sum of all their parts, so if they have something you want and you envy them for having it, you must first be willing to take on everything that's happened to them up to the point that they got what you want.
- This also means you must give up everything in your life that's caused you to be the "who" who you are today.
- Yes, you get to give up all the pains, all the injustices, all the trauma you've suffered. You must also give up any joys, any happinesses, any love, any children, any friends, any lovers you've experienced because these also caused you to be the "who" who you are.

Decide carefully, I said. Your life, both joys and sorrows, got you to a place where you could have this conversation. Are you willing to give it all up? I've known people who've had the most hellish lives imaginable yet state freely that if it weren't for people they met, they wouldn't be alive. Others (myself included) have said "I wouldn't want to repeat my life, nor would I want to change it."

So decide carefully.

You get to have all their joys but you must give up all your joys. You get to give up all your sorrows but you must take on all their sorrows.

How will you decide?

Breaking Up Can Be a Killer and Other Ways to Add/Remove Years from your Life

People are impressed when I mention that NextStage (see Appendix: Definitions) is completing a ten or fifteen year study. They're more impressed when I reference studies of ten to twenty year durations as "starts".

An example of a study with enough basis to provide reliable results to me is "The Longevity Project". It's an eighty — 8 0 — year study of what contributes to a long, happy life.

Eighty years in the making? I've known people who didn't live that long. Maybe there's some things in here we should pay attention to?

Like men having a tougher time during and after a divorce than women do. This finding doesn't truly surprise me. Male and female support networks are based on different interaction models. Males experience greater challenges finding social happiness than women do, and that's just for starters.

How about working long and hard is more healthful than playing all the time. There are two take aways for yours truly in this: I'm going to live a very long life and I wonder how being a professional games-player or sportsperson works in. I've known some professionals in sports and gaming and at their level it is work, often long and hard, so I guess it balances out.

And exercise isn't the cure all many think it is. Does this mean I can give up Pilates? My instructor, who we lovingly call "The Empress Brutalia of the Pilates People", will disagree and I know I fit into my clothes better than before, so I'll continue.

Do you know conscientious, meticulous, thoughtful people? Are they in better, happier marriages, have stronger and more friendships and more pleasant and rewarding work situations? They should be, according to this study.

Are you a woman in a traditionally masculine occupation? Chances are you're going to take a few years off your life. Ditto for males.

But if you're a male in a traditionally female occupation, you'll live longer. And women doing "women's work" will, too.

But wait a second

This study was eighty years in the taking. Add another five or so in the making. That means the people studied lived remarkably different lives from us. Up to half their lives were without TV, probably a quarter without radio or telephone and most likely they didn't use the internet, email, mobiles, etc., until their last years.

Women didn't have occupation options similar to — not identical to, that hasn't happened yet, me thinks — men's until ... oh ... mid-1980s, maybe? Again, that was later in the lives of lots of these people.

And any study started that long ago probably involved selection prejudices — I know, hard to believe that studies started 90+ years ago would be subject to racial, ethnic, etc., prejudices — that definitely skew the results.

All the above is true. Still, there's stuff to be learned. Or investigated further.

And it's still a fascinating read.

How Do You Define "Love"?

Long, long ago in internet time (okay, back in 2005 or so), a personals/online dating company came to NextStage (see Appendix: Definitions) and asked if we could create a tool — a Love Gauge — that would tell if people were a good match for each other, i.e., would fall in love. Even better, could the tool determine how long lasting that relationship would be. We responded, "How do you define Love?"

There are three basic kinds of Love

Humans are capable of three basic forms of love: Agape, Philios and Eros (I'm writing about recognizable differences in how the brain registers "love." Some authors write about Philautia, Storge, and others. Such may exist in literature and counseling sessions, not in brain wiring. Sorry). Most people can figure out Eros pretty quickly: it's the ritualization of reproductive sex. I write "ritualization" from a cultural anthropology perspective. Our brains' most powerful circuitry, the neuroanatomical pieces that will win every argument every time, still

rule our lives in this order:
1. Can I survive?
2. Can I mate?
3. Can I eat?

People are amazed at how much time our non-conscious minds devote to ensuring those three things can happen. All that talk about altruism and giving one's life for another? Those are easily explained by behavioral ethology. All that talk about fidelity? Look to cultural anthropology. Making sure everyone has enough and the right things to eat? Watch the Food Channel.

So Eros, erotic love, is pretty much physical in demonstration and mental in causation. Humans need to think sexually in order to intentionally perform sexually and the former, the thinking, must always take place first.

Philios is the "higher" form of love and the term from which Philadelphia, "The City of Brotherly Love", gets its name. Philios is the love we have for our family, our friends, our neighbors and so on. On a cognitive level, are there things you'd do for your friends that you wouldn't do for your lovers or vice versa? If yes, those differences are demonstrations of how you consciously and non-consciously segment Eros from Philios.

Agape is the love "God has for man" and is actually recognized in two forms, top down — God to us — and bottom up. The love we have for our chosen deities is the "bottom up" form of agape love. Not only that, but the "love" we have for country, for causes, for institutions, for groups, et cetera, all fall into the agape category. Whenever we believe there's a "love" relationship between us and something we recognize as "greater" than us, it is coming from the parts of the brain that register and respond to agape love. The emotions a toddler has for their parent, recognizably older siblings and adult near-family members (grandmas and grandpas, aunts and uncles, etc.) is agape in nature, growing into philios (we hope) as they mature.

Part of human neural design is that we are capable of experiencing these three loves separately, simultaneously, and in all mixtures possible.

It's wonderful, how we're designed.

Back to Making Tools

The company that wanted a Love Gauge was, it turned out, primarily interested in Eros and Philios, and they weren't particular which one dominated at what point in the relationship so long as people were satisfied with their partnerings long enough not to blame this company should a relationship turn sour.

Our tools' technology base currently is capable of recognizing agape and philios, but not eros.

Darn, huh?

So we told them that. We shook hands and walked away.

But not before we developed a Compatibility Gauge. We developed the Compatibility Gauge because we thought going through the motions would help us figure out how to recognize and measure eros.

Well, it didn't.

But then I got a call from a friend who's also a regular client in a completely unrelated industry, one that builds on and offline communities. We got to talking about recent projects and I mentioned NextStage's Compatibility Gauge ("NSCG" for short). I explained philios and agape to him and he said, "So it can determine if two people will get along, just not if they'll fall in love, right?"

Yep.

"Can it determine if two groups will get along?" Yep.

"How about someone coming into an existing workgroup. Could it determine if they'll fit in and contribute?" Definitely.

"How about if someone would be a good manager for an existing team?" Yup.

"Can it determine if two companies should merge?" To a point, yes.

"How about if someone would be a good CEO for an existing company?" Ayup.

"Brands and fans?" Yes. "Brand persona and Consumer Persona?"

Yes.

"So it can figure out who should be accepted into a particular branded community for testing purposes?" Yep, sure can.

Not to mention who'd make good political running mates. Or who'd be good friends.

And thus a tool was born.

But wait, there's more ...

A while later (a long while later in internet terms) I was talking with someone else and they made an offhand comment that got me to thinking about a way to modify one of our existing tools, NextStage OnSite, NSOS. NSOS traditionally reported on website visitors en masse, not individually. It could determine group behavior and response but wasn't designed to report on individuals.

But what they said gave me an idea of how to modify the math inside that tool so that it could report on certain elements of individual behaviors.

Modifying NSOS brought me again to a Love Gauge concept. There had to be a way to do it, I simply wasn't understanding the problem correctly.

So I asked our technology "What is Love between two people?"

First, yes, we can actually ask our technology such things and get an understandable response. Second, because our technology currently "thinks" like a child albeit a child with a vast knowledge of how humans interact, it responded with

- Eros: Pleasurable compassionate attention to another's person
- Philios: Consistent demonstrations that another's peace and understanding have equal value to the self's peace and understanding
- Agape: Trust beyond knowledge, understanding, and experience

We've gotten used to our technology being Zen-like and Koanish. For example, "Pleasureable compassionate attention to another's person" makes quite a bit of sense when one breaks the phrase up a bit:

"Be aware of their physical, emotional and psychological pleasure/pain thresholds and move between them as they wish. Focus more on them than on yourself."

That "Be aware of their physical, emotional and psychological pleasure/pain thresholds and move between them as they wish. Focus more on them than on yourself" is actually something our technology can measure and report on because love, regardless of the form, is more about the mind than the body and a lot of what's in that definition is mind-based, not body-based.

We've gotten used to our technology being smarter than us.

What Kind of Lover Are You (And Can You Improve)?

Once upon a time at NextStage (see Appendix: Definitions), we created a love-determining tool: NextStage LoveJones.

That name, *LoveJones*, comes from a friend. We are forever in her debt. She is assured someone she knows will claim "NextStage LoveJones proves what I've been telling my wife for years!" We've already heard much the same from a user in Texas.

Anyway …

So how does one determine if you, right at this moment sitting there reading this book, perhaps while you're commuting via train, subway, bus or taxi, maybe in a plane waiting for it to take-off or even if you're in-flight and you're reading this stored on your tablet or phone, are a good lover?

Turns out it's pretty easy once you understand what's involved, and what's involved in a love based relationship was described (for our purposes) in "How Do You Define 'Love'?".

Defining Love

To recap, it's much more than physical (something most people immediately think of and rarely admit it's the first thing they think of). There's the attention before and after, the emotional energy that is subtly based on physicality and is often spawned by a simple touch, look or smile, the psychological energy that comes from familial, social, cultural, and tribal alliances, and the spiritual energy that comes from all of these things blending together. As one early reader of this post offered, "Love is doing things together and allowing things to be done separately."

I wrote that love in any form starts in the head before it's demonstrated by the heart, the hands, the words, et cetera, in "How Do You Define 'Love'?". This "head before heart, et cetera" is true for all of the higher emotions.

What are "higher emotions"?

Higher emotions are more easily described by starting at the bottom — or at least lower end — of the emotional spectrum.

Lower (or "Primitive") emotions tend to work along survival axes. Probably the best known of these axes is *Flight or Fight* and all of these axes deal with the sympathetic versus parasympathetic nervous systems.

Lower emotions are housed in our primitive (what some call "reptilian") brain regions and if you've ever jumped at a loud noise or felt your heart pound after a boom of thunder or leapt out of the way when you see a teenager driving a car, you've experienced a *primal response* and have your lower emotions to thank. Animals demonstrate lower emotions all the time. We may want to believe our pets love us and the behavioral ethology of it is they recognize us as part of their pack, their pride, their flock, their mate, whatever, and even when we're the alphas in the pride, pack or flock, their behavior towards us has more to do with group harmony than individual affection.

The higher emotions are a bit more complex and involved, and the obvious axes get a little convoluted. For example, ask most people what the opposite of Love is and they'll answer Hate and that's not accurate. Both Love and Hate are strong emotions and are usually directed at something or someone. The opposite of a strong emotion is neutrality, indifference, a lack of concern, interest or caring, so the opposite of both love and hate is apathy.

But the interesting thing about lower and higher emotions is the latter are built on the former. That's how our brains evolved, both figuratively and literally, both in our own lives from children to adults and as a species from pampas to homeowner.

Love, it turns out, is an excellent example of that evolvement from lower/primitive to higher as indicated in "How Do You Define 'Love'?"

How Love Evolved

What we now recognize as "love" started out as quite primitive, quite low, and through eons of evolution that low, primitive emotion has become what we now call *Eros* or erotic love. Yes, that heart thumping, gland morphing, secondary sexual attribute defining I-gotta-get-me-some sweat-involving thang is the latest incarnation of one of biology's greatest triumphs, survival of the species.

Survival of the species is so important to us that evolution rewards erotic love with intense pleasure (for most of us. One of my favorite quotes is "Sex, done right, is very, very good. And even when done poorly it can still be very, very good.")

Survival-of-the-species love took a step up the evolutionary ladder due to our ancestors developing social brains. That step up the ladder is *Philios*. We still want to ensure survival of our species, we're simply diversifying our investment. The lion's share still goes to our own progeny and thanks to Philios we'll now give some of our share to those in our group, tribe, society, culture, nation, race, ... Philios or "Brotherly Love" is why we'll stick up for *us* and go to war against *them*. We, as a group, tribe, society, et cetera, survive thanks to philios.

The next step up the evolutionary ladder was literally a step upward and is *Agape* love, the love we feel for nation, for deity, for those things recognizably larger than ourselves. Once our social brain caused us to seek out others of our kind, the next step was to recognize the strongest unifying form of Philios was philios for a specific One rather than philios for each other. This enabled us to become further philiatic by deciding our One was better than their One. Philios becoming agape results in the most horrible wars because the bloodiest, most devastating, genocidal crimes and conflicts are religious and/or belief-based.

Love Fascinates Me

"Love" has fascinated me since I was a child, literally. I asked my grandparents why they loved each other, I asked my parents what love was and how did they know they were in love. I asked my cousin the night before his wedding how he knew this she was the right she and have asked friends how they met, fell in love and what keeps them in love.

So NextStage, thanks to my early interest in such matters, has more than twenty years' research conducted all over the world, in societies primitive and modern and all those in between, regarding love.

We compared the results of that research to what our technology had determined previously (see "How Do You Define 'Love'?") and made adjustments as necessary.

And thanks to a breakthrough in neuromathematics that we stumbled upon earlier this year, we created a tool to determine how good a lover someone was likely to be. All we had to do was trigger a signal along the aforementioned evolutionary trail and follow where it led.

Then we tested. That was the fun part.

We had to test with people who could be objective about themselves, people who didn't let their desires, their egos, their own wants and needs, their self-concepts, … get in the way of considering if the results were valid.

Or if the results indicated ways they could improve.

The Most Important Sex Organ

The most important sex organ is the brain according to Regina Brett. We recognize this as "what happens in the head is echoed in the body and what happens in the body is echoed in the head." That evolutionary trail that goes from body to brain is where all the different nervous systems (there's quite a few, really) get involved and climbing up and down the emotional evolutionary ladder becomes obvious.

Let me give you an example of something happening in the brain and being echoed in the body. Imagine you're sitting comfortably in your home watching a documentary on warcrimes and see something extremely disturbing. You may look away and some people might change the channel. But what is "disturbing" is learned. What's disturbing to a native New Englander might be completely ignored by a Sudanese and vice versa. Thus the turning away or changing channels — the physical demonstration — occurs because the brain/mind a) have been taught what the (culturally) acceptable response is and then b) decided whether to act upon that teaching in this instance.

Now let's consider something happening in the body and being echoed in the mind. Have you ever had a bad cold? You've got the shivers and shakes, you're coughing and sneezing, and it's difficult to concentrate on anything more involved than gameshows and Oprah. The stresses on the body affect the brain/mind's ability to function optimally and we want nothing more than to sit under a blanket in front of a blazing fire.

Thus what happens in the body is echoed in the mind, what happens in the mind is echoed in the body. People observe these little echoes all the time and respond to them accordingly. It's how we know someone's depressed just by looking at them, that someone else is having a good or bad day, that someone's probably lying to us while someone else is telling us the truth and so on. We don't directly comment on these observations usually, and most people observe and respond to them nonconsciously after a certain age. They essentially forget about them and simply act upon them.

Ah, But At NextStage...

... we take great advantage of such things, especially the non-conscious things, the little things people do that they are unaware they're doing. NextStage observed these behaviors consciously and with intention and has developed a patented technology to observe and report on them.

Breadcrumbs

Let me give you an example of what's been going on starting with this post's title, "What Kind of Lover Are You?" The human psyche (under normal circumstances) will answer a question when asked one. There may be no verbal response and there will be a response, one perhaps spoken only to one's self in one's mind. Asking such a question is an example of priming. The response to the question is actually demonstrated in the body (unless you've had a lot of highly specific and usually individualized training, and I'm guessing the majority of readers haven't) and ET detects that response.

In fact, if you go back over this post you'll see there are lots of questions:

- How Do You Define Love?
- So how does one determine if you ... are a good lover?
- How Do You Define Love? again
- How Do You Define Love? yet again
- What are "higher emotions"?
- How Do You Define Love? one more time
- How Do You Define Love? #5
- Have you ever had a bad cold?
- How Do You Define Love? for the almost last time

The first thing you should notice is the core question, "How do you define 'love'?", is asked six times before this line you're currently reading. The rest of the questions are embedded in text that will cause specific brain areas — memory, cognitive resources, limbic system, visual centers, the PNI, ... the list is pretty long. We designed this material to hit a lot of things. For that matter when this was a blog post we incorporated the surrounding ads, fluff and bluff into the neural registrations — to fire at different times.

Each firing causes subtle, not easily recognizable yet easily recordable changes in the body. These subtle changes aren't recognizable because modern society teaches its members to not pay attention to them any longer, which is a pity because being able to recognize and respond to such changes ensured our survival throughout our evolutionary history.

Ever feel uncomfortable in some situation and find out (usually) too late you're in psychological, social, emotional, or perhaps even physical danger? Ever tell yourself or someone "I had a hunch … " or "I thought that was going to happen" or something along those lines? Congrats! That was your non-conscious (which is still quite aware of these changes even though your consciousness isn't) nudging you in the back (and should you be interested in learning how to recognize such changes consciously, sign up for my That Think You Do classes (See the end of the book for more on classes)).

Back to love. Learn and recognize these changes and you'll immediately, consciously recognize things about yourself and those around you such as "Oh, my gosh! I'm falling in love" versus "Oh, my gosh! I'm falling in lust" and the same for those around you.

And getting back to evolutionary survival skills, you'll be able to recognize when someone is faking their love and affection before you and they end up in court or somewhere equally displeasing.

Intention

I've been studying people who are "living with intention" for about twenty-five years now. Originally I found them due to my cultural anthropology studies. Now I'm finding a few of them in the modern world.

"Living with intention?" you ask. "What does that mean, exactly?"

Hmm ... the simple answer is "*Living with Intention* means paying attention to everything you do" and that's so weak, so minimal, that only a western trained mind would offer it, so I apologize.

It means being in the moment ... while appreciating (not quite, not exactly. English is limited in its ability to express this concept. Or I am limited in my ability to express this concept) ... *feeling*? ... every moment that came before you and will come after you.

It means doing whatever you're doing as if the fate of the universe hung in the balance ... while being able to laugh at yourself regardless of the outcome.

It means focusing all your attention on each individual task ... while being aware of everything else that's going on around you (and recognizing that "around you" can be very, very big).

It means taking complete and ultimate joy in everything you do … while understanding it may be the last thing you do.

It means being aware of everything going on around, in, and through you each and every moment … and being at peace with it — not necessarily enjoying it or hating it, just being at peace with it, accepting it (because there's a difference between liking something and accepting something).

And this list gets longer and longer and longer the more I attempt to put into words what can only happen deep inside the individual (because part of intention is being able to keep two completely opposite thoughts in your mind simultaneously, penecontemporaneously).

As one of my teachers said to me, "I can help you find your door. Only you can open your door and walk through. But walking through, there's no walking back."

Brushing your teeth.

Pay attention to what you're doing. To how you're doing it. Be aware of the feel of the brush in your hand and the bristles on your teeth and the taste of the toothpaste and the brush's movement on your gums and … and be so aware of the fact that you're doing all this that it becomes a game to you, something to delight in, something to rejoice in, something to be thankful for, to be prayerful about.

But those last words imply something religious and nothing about being intentful is religious. Sufis live with intent but sufism isn't religious in philosophy, only as it is practiced by some.

Some will read this and think, "Oh, Zen," and while lots of zen practitioners live with intent the former doesn't imply the latter. Some will think "Oh, Yin Yang" and to think that demonstrates not knowing, a lack of understanding.

Some of the people I've studied have been Catholic, some Baptist, some Lutheran, some Evangelical, some Jewish, some agnostic, some pagan, some aboriginal, some Sufi, some shamanic, some Hindi, some Muslim, some native american, some Buddhist, some …

I have noticed commonalities. Regardless of anything else, they're all remarkable listeners. They're all remarkably patient, kind and giving. They all have incredible boundaries. They're self-aware in ways most people can't imagine.

Imagine kissing someone simultaneously passionately and casually, kind of like kissing your partner when you see each other, a gentle "hello I missed you today" kiss, yet having all your feelings about that person, all your desires and hopes for them, all your wanting of them, delivered in that little, possibly public kiss.

I'm writing this and recognizing that I could be writing this with intention, too.

Everything slows down. I focus on each word, each phrase, each expression. I recognize what's important before I type the words themselves.

I focus on what I'm doing so I can also focus on what you're doing. Will you slow down? Will you read with intent?

When you wake up tomorrow, will your first thoughts be that the day is yours, completely yours, to do with what you will, truly Carpe Diem and that your first thoughts dictate whether you seize the day or the day seizes you?

I have been practicing living with intent. It's not easy for me. I screw up quite a bit and blame it on this modern world. Yet I know others who are living intentionally and are in this same modern world I am in; they're not living in communities where everyone is devoted to intentional living and each person helps each other person live intentionally.

For myself, the moments when I do it are like the best physical exercise — a definite sense of exertion along with a sense of fulfillment, of well being, of peace. An endorphin rush for the mind, emotions and spirit.

Living with intention takes commitment. And acceptance. I accept that my mistakes are merely part of appreciating my commitment to living with intention. From those I study I know the recognizable commitment fades because the commitment becomes part of the intent.

Where does a wise person hide a pebble? On a beach. Where does a wise person hide a leaf? In a forest.

Eat Better or Be Stupid, Your Choice

Disney has made public that they won't tolerate junk food — high sugars, high carbs, low protein, poor health — advertising on their media channels, in their parks and resorts, on their cruise ships, …

The reach is impressive.

It's also not surprising that Disney (and others) would make such a move. The amount of press letting us know how poor our dietary habits are is amazing. Thank goodness the insurance industry has realized that it's cheaper to insure people with good dietary habits than people with poor dietary habits. And thank goodness the food&beverage industry has figured out how to make money off of (relatively) healthy foods&beverages.

I mean, you don't think there'd be this media oriented public outcry if such wasn't the case, do you?

Knowledge of the devastating health affects of poor diet, too much sugar when we're too young, so on and so forth has been in the scientific literature for quite some time. It's nothing new. It only seems to be new because companies have figured out how to make money off it.

Jaded? Moi? N'est-ce pas!

But Did You Know Poor Diets Make You Stupid?

Okay, a bit of an overstatement. I'm taking a cue from the insurance and food&beverage industries to make old knowledge seem brightly new and shiny.

Never-the-less, it has been established that high-calorie diets lead to poor memory function and a host of other concerns. Most striking was that just a brief foray into fats and sugars can cause a little disorientation — the next time you want a beer and pizza, get it delivered. You may not be able to find your way home.

Memory problems and disorientation tend to manifest rapidly. Cognitive loss also occurs although it takes longer. Imagine knowing something's wrong but not being able to remember what to do about it. And all this occurs long before high calorie foods appear as body weight gains.

Forget "Once passed the lips, forever on the hips", we're talking about "Once passed the lips … I can't remember the rest."

So the next time you want to sit down with a bag of peanut M&Ms or a half-gallon of ice cream, get a couple of celery stalks instead.

If nothing else, at least you'll remember where you put the M&Ms and ice cream. Eat the M&Ms and ice cream first and you may not be able to find the celery.

No Brain, No Gain (or something like that)

I know a fellow who never tires of telling me what great new brain training site he's visited. He uses their free training tools then puts down a few dollars for whatever's behind door #2, so to speak.

"These really help you?"

"I'm thinking a lot better than I was before," he tells me enthusiastically.

"How do you know?"

"They have tests you can take. Some of these sites won't let you go to the next level unless you pass their tests."

I just stared, waiting for the punch line. Eventually I supplied it. "And that next level costs just a few dollars more, I'll bet."

"Of course it does. You don't think they're going to let you use their training program for free, do you?"

(now wait for it)

"And the tests cost you something?"

"Well duh yes, of course!"

Budda thump!

I'm not the only one who's skeptical about these things. It turns out researchers in Britain and for the BBC also had questions about these brain training sites. They worked with individuals who performed online tasks over six weeks. The amount of work varied but the base was ten minutes a day, three times a week for six weeks.

This was a massive study, the kind that can only be done longitudinally (in the real world) or virtually (online). Over 10,000 people took part ranging in age from 18 to 60.

And you know what?

No noticeable improvements. Not a one. Nothing obvious.

Did the study participants recognize any effects?

Nothing that correlated to the study.

Most researchers in this field agree that more studies have to be performed before any final conclusions can be drawn.

But there's no doubt that these *brain training* companies have learned how to make money off people.

Maybe I should sign up?

Framing Decisions

This post is about the intersection of two usually minor things. Gnats, really. Annoyances and not much more. Things you'd just as soon swat as put any real effort into.

However, when they come together and they often do, they come together like two freight trains colliding in the night.

We're talking way beyond dangerous here.

Vulnerable

Have you ever had a day when you felt just a little "out of sorts"? A tad discombobulated, perhaps? You're just not firing on all cylinders and you know it? You're a little off, maybe?

There are lots of signs you're feeling this way even if you don't recognize them as such: you take things more seriously than you should. You take things the wrong way. You're more sensitive to others' opinions. Jokes aren't as funny as they should be. You're melancholy. You feel a little cold even though everyone else is perfectly comfortable. You deny yourself simple pleasures - a stick of gum, a piece of candy, that last cup of coffee - for no real reason you can think of. Things like that.

The common term for this malaise is *vulnerability*. Everybody has vulnerable moments. It's normal, even healthy. There's lots of reasons for a sense of vulnerability. The best thing to do when you feel vulnerable is take a moment and figure out what's causing it. There's always a reason. Sometimes you've caught a cold or the flu and it hasn't completely manifested yet. Sometimes your stomach's upset but not enough to knock you out. Ditto a headache. Other times it can be something that's happened or happening in your life. A friend is moving away, a raise doesn't come, a relationship ends or begins. Perhaps a bad night's sleep, or dreams that left you feeling a little off.

Whatever the cause, take a moment and see if you can figure out what's making you feel vulnerable. Often being able to point your finger at the cause of feeling vulnerable is enough to make it go away.

Decisions

Have you ever had a day when you need to make a decision? Doesn't matter if it's minor or major, it can be anywhere from "Should I have another cup of coffee?" to "Should I relocate my family for that job?"

All that matters is it's a decision that has emotional elements and is more than a logical "Yes/No" type question.

Train Wreck

Feelings of vulnerability can be thought of as mild or minor depressive episodes. Everybody has them and they're only a concern when they either don't go away or they escalate. What's important for this discussion is that they're *depressive*, meaning different parts of your brain and different aspects of your conscious and non-conscious selves are not communicating optimally. No where near it, in fact.

You are, in a sense, *under the influence* of a self-generated narcotic, hypnotic, soporific, take your pick.

The point is, you're not in any condition to make a decision of any kind. You're literally not in the right *frame* of mind to make a *decision*.

Make a decision when you feel vulnerable and your decision will be based on avoidance of pain, not on attracting pleasure. You'll be making a decision in a depressive state, you won't be thinking clearly, and your sense of vulnerability will cause you to act emotionally, not logically. You'll flame someone you could just as easily ignore, you'll say something you shouldn't to someone you care about or who cares for you, you'll be less kind when you could be more.

It's amazing what a little vulnerability can do to our lives.

Looking Both Ways Before Crossing the Intersection

Fortunately, there are some simple fixes for avoiding such train wrecks and they all begin with *self-awareness*. Literally, do you feel or sense something's amiss?

Then stop what you're doing until things pass (and they will). Meetings can usually be postponed, phone calls can be rescheduled, projects can be delayed an hour or even a day with little to no difficulty.

Quite simply, when you sense something's amiss, take a moment and see if there's any decisions you need to make. Most will be minor and can be postponed until your vulnerability passes.

Is there something truly important that can't wait? Ask a trusted friend or co-worker's advice and help. Strategize with them. Listen, pay attention, seek input and feedback. Is this person truly trusted? Tell them you're feeling vulnerable. They'll understand and help you through it. Most times just talking it through with someone helps to put things in perspective and you become aware of what's causing the vulnerability so you can deal with it.

So the next time you're feeling vulnerable and have to make a decision, don't.

That intersection is a dangerous one to cross. Look both ways then look again.

Chances are you'll figure out what's bothering you, be able to chuckle and shrug it off, then make the decision with a clear mind and heart. The greatest benefit is that you'll be in better control of your life. You'll be able to appreciate and deal with your moods rather than be dictated by them. No small achievement, that.

The Stranger The Better

A fascinating piece of social research has made it to my desk. It deals with males' success rate with females in typical mating situations.

To readers outside of social anthropology, this means "What can guys do to make sure girls notice them in bars, at clubs, in the mall, in the hall, in the cafeteria, at the dance, ... ?"

The research points out one of those things that's obvious. So obvious, one might ask, "Somebody had to do research on this?"

Well, yes. Because when you think about it, it's not what most guys do in typical mating situations and that's probably why few males have the kind of success they want.

The Trick Is

Be a little different from your mates, your buddies, your pals, whatever you want to call them, when you go out as a group. Or if you're not going out as a group, be a little different than most other guys when you go out where other males will be.

For example, wear flashy suspenders with bright accessories on otherwise drab, run of the mill clothing. Or a different kind of hat. Or a clown nose.

The trick is to get women to look, even for a second because that one second puts you one second ahead of the ... umm ... competition.

Women may not flock to you and they will, generally, be more receptive should you approach them.

It Works Because

It turns out that women of all ages cue to the different in mating situations. Neuroscience uses the term "difference sorters" for this and it means that, given one-hundred things that are all the same and only one thing among those hundred that are different, females as a group will devote attention to the one different thing before they'll pay attention to any one of the one-hundred similar things. Evolution has designed them to look for the one perfect jaw and good teeth (for example) among all the other jaws and teeth because that one perfect jaw and good teeth meant a good hunter, good provider, and better genetic material for her offspring (than the hundred other fellows with common jaws and teeth), meaning her genes had a better than average chance of survival, too.

Those evolutionary factors are still hard at work even though the pampas or forest or mountains have been replaced by malls, dance halls, cafeterias, offices, and so on.

So if you're just a little different — not a lot different — females will notice you and make a mental note that you're interesting.

Specifically, they will note that you're more interesting than the other males around you.

And guys, in case you haven't figured it out yet, being interesting works really well when it comes to attracting females. Nice cars, big bankroll, great job, expensive clothes, great bling, these are all good things too, no question about it.

Of course, they're good because they're interesting. Especially when your competition doesn't have them. Such things make you ...

umm ... different.

Here's What You Can't Do

Different is nice and it has to be different within certain boundaries. You can't land your hovercraft in the company parking lot and expect to get the kind of attention you want. You'll get attention, I'm sure, simply not the kind you want from females you'd want interested in you.

You can't wear gold like Mr. T in his heyday if you're going to a friend's moving party.

Be different, yes, but be different within the setting's limits. Stand out enough to be seen, not stared at.

You'll do fine.

Lohginess Begone! (Personal Inventories)

Have you ever had a day where you couldn't get out of your own way? A day where, no matter what you did, your mind was fixed on stuff that kept you down and out? It might have started with something someone said or something someone did or didn't do, and in the end, your gumption deficit was all you, *you*, **you**!

Just the thing you want to hear when you're in one of those moods, isn't it?

There's a term for that mood you're in. Some people call it "being glum", we prefer the term "lohgi" (pronounced LOW-gee with a hard "g") because "lohgi" sounds more like what you feel than "glum" does.

"Glum" sounds like you're stuck in something and can't move, "lohgi" sounds like you're moving but can't get up any momentum so no matter what you're doing, you're doing it slow. And without enthusiasm. An important part of "lohgi" is the lack of enthusiasm. "Glum" has that "lack of enthusiasm" sound but if you can't move you're basically exhausting yourself for no reason. At least with "lohgi" you're moving so things can change.

If you know how to change them.

First Trick - Practice When You Don't Need This Trick

The worst thing you can do to battle glumness and/or lohginess is attempt to fight it barehanded when it's already won.

So don't.

Instead, when you're having a great day, when things are completely going your way and life is grand, take a few seconds and ask yourself, "Why are things so good right now?"

Answer yourself with a list, what's called a *Personal Inventory*. For example, did you sleep well the night before? Did you have a great conversation with a friend or coworker? Did you see a movie or video that made you smile? Did the love of your life tell you that you were the love of their life?

The reasons you could be having an incredible, one-off, completely over-the-top day are likely uncountable, so just make a list of two to five and keep it in your pocket, on your mobile, on your tablet, as a screensaver, whatever. Just make sure that wherever you put that list, it's handy and reachable for you.

Now do this again the next time you're having an incredible, wonderful, or even slightly better than average day. Okay, do it for even your average days.

Do it until your list has about twenty or so different items on it. And keep it handy.

Putting Practice into Play

What you've done is teach yourself to catalog your emotional state. The above teaches you to catalog your positive emotional states.

Now, when you get glum or lohgi, do the same thing; catalog your emotional state and this time, create a personal inventory of why things are so lohgi.

Compare and Contrast

Got that first list handy? Great. Now compare it to your lohgi list. What you're looking for are items on the positive list that are missing from the lohgi list. This is about learning what causes you to be lohgi and what causes you to be happy, not which list has more entries.

Ask yourself, right there in the middle of your lohginess and while you're looking at your lists, what's different and what's made things different. Pick one or two things that are different and make sure they're from the same list - either one or two things from the positive list or one or two things from the lohgi list.

Pick a Direction and Go

Consider those one or two things that are different. Are the one or two things from your positive list? Then consciously move towards them. This may mean emotionally, it may mean physically, spiritually, mentally, or some combination, doesn't matter, all that matters is that you move towards them.

Are they from your lohgi list? Then consciously move away from them. Emotionally, physically, spiritually, mentally or some combination thereof, doesn't matter, move yourself away from whatever you've picked from your lohgi list.

That's why "lohgi" is better than "glum". You're moving anyway, may as well move in a direction that'll help you than sit there being stuck and unable to do anything about it.

Don't you think?

Finishing

A recent discussion with some friends led to interesting places. It started with "What gives you the most pleasure?"

Some answered a quiet evening at home, a walk in the park, being at the seaside. Others offered a book so captivating the world went away while they were reading. A few offered a favorite piece of music (some playing, some listening). A good meal with good friends because it didn't matter how good the food, the service, the restaurant, et cetera, was, it was being among friends that mattered.

One fellow, Terry, smiled and nodded as the others spoke. His hands rested on top of the table and toyed with an opened straw beside his drink. I noticed he kept his eyes closed and his breathing slowed to the point I thought he fell asleep.

The others finished sharing and the conversation shifted to weekend plans.

I held up my hand. "Wait a second, Terry hasn't answered yet. You don't have to answer, Terry, I just want to make sure you have a chance if you'd like to answer."

Terry chuckled. Terry's a big, balding man with a surprising tenor voice. His chuckle is musical.

He opened his eyes but didn't lift them from the straw and the table top. "Finishing," he said.

Jack, sitting next to me and across from Terry, frowned. "Finishing what?"

"Doesn't matter. Finishing."

His quiet, reflective answer made me curious. "Could you share some more?"

He shrugged and adjusted himself in his chair. The waiter exchanged our empty plates for coffee cups. "Anything else?"

We were all good. He left. Terry shrugged a second time. "I wrote a novel."

I knew. Not sure how many others did. Terry's always been shy about it.

What is necessary at this point is to know that Terry's run three marathons, been a top-level executive at Coca-Cola, ATT, and a few others, started his own real estate company which is currently one of the largest in a major metropolitan area, grew it until he became an investor, and started a commercial real estate division. He's in a great relationship, raised a wonderful daughter who's constantly making the dean's list, and is on the boards of several charitable institutions. In his late fifties, Terry's built quite the resume.

Jack laughed. "Another feather in your cap, bro?"

Terry shook his head. "The only feather."

The others checked their watches. Time to get back to whatever. I stayed. "The only feather?"

"I've had lots of successes, sure. I started writing a novel in my early twenties but put it away because I didn't think I could."

"Some things take time to complete."

"No, everything else I did? I did to cover up my failure at not finishing that novel."

I nodded. Compensation guilt.

Many successful people mask their failure in one area by

excelling in other areas. They'll mask fears, mask identity concerns, ... Compensation guilt also shows up in other parts of life; the partner who gifts their significant other after an argument, the parent who spends extra time with a child after missing a game or other event, the boss who treats their staff to a lunch or dinner after an unwarranted outburst, ... , all are examples of compensation guilt.

One area where compensation guilt is publicly demonstrated is in sports, and perhaps the greatest known example is Kaitlyn Jenner's story about winning five gold olympic medals as Bruce Jenner and excelling in several aggressive/assertive male activities. All were done to compensate for then-Bruce's inability to express his true self.

Terry shared his business and sports successes were to hide his shame and guilt at not doing what he really wanted to do, finish his novel.

Let me be clear on this. Publicly recognized success is gratifying. The appreciation of one's peers for a job well-done is good for the mind, body, spirit, and emotion.

But having that recognition and not believing you deserve it, knowing you still have a hole inside which success after success after success can't fill, is deadening rather than enlivening.

Some Helpful Success Goals

Personal successes - the kind which give us a sense of inner fulfillment - can be single elements of the success we're working towards. Here are some examples:
1. You want to learn to play the piano and are frustrated because Bach's Toccata and Fugue in D minor eludes you. Practice one measure until you've mastered it. Next practice the last notes of the measure you just mastered and the first notes of the next measure until the transition between measures is seamless. Now practice the rest of the next measure immediately upon practicing the transition. Eventually you'll play the entire piece (and I'll be jealous).

2. You want to take up jogging or running with the goal of entering a 5k race. Start by walking one kilometer. Next walk that one kilometer briskly. Now start walking and after twenty steps jog twenty. Repeat this twenty-for-twenty until you complete the kilometer comfortably. Now do twenty-for-forty, twenty-for-eighty, ... Add the second kilometer. Now jog the first kilometer and do twenty-for the second, the third, the fourth, ... Do this every day and you'll be doing 5k races by the end of the month.
3. You want to get out of debt, have three credit cards with balances of $5k, $2k, and $500 respectively. Many people put their money towards the $5k bill in the hopes of knocking it down with the end result of charging on the other two until those catch up.

A better strategy is to pay off the $500 card. It requires less money, can be done quickly, and you'll have the satisfaction of succeeding in lowering your debt. The other cards can then be paid off as well with the money originally going towards the $500 balance.

This single element methodology works because it breaks large tasks into easily manageable, easily succeedable small tasks.

How did Terry finish his novel (he's now had three published)?

He wrote a page at a time until it was done.

Appendix: Principles

What follows is a living document. Things are added. To date (45+ years), nothing's been deleted. Some comes from things my Grandfather taught me, some from life, some from my own studies, journeys, and what have you. A friend, learning much came from my Grandfather, nodded and congratulated me for keeping my Grandpa's teaching alive. "We've lost the elements of honoring the elders," she said.

Someone once asked me if I've lived up to the Principles myself.

"Hell no. That's why I write them down. So they can be a guide to me, so I'll know when I am not following them."

Like so much in my life, they are for me. If others benefit from them, wonderful (and it seems many do). But first and foremost, they are for me.

You may not like them all. You may only be comfortable with one or two.

Good start. Work to integrate them all. Find that difficult? As noted above, if they were easy for me to follow I wouldn't write them down.

I will offer you can't pick and choose. Or at least it seems most people can't. I haven't met anyone who's done so successfully, known many who have tried and failed.

One fellow studied them for a while and told me he couldn't find any contradictions in them. They seem internally consistent.

Reassuring, that.

"Does that mean you'll follow them?"

"No way. I've got a life to live."

And so it goes.

1. Do unto others as if they were you.

In other words, cut out the middle man. Treat others the way you treat yourself. People do this anyway. All we do is suggest you become aware of it.

2. Trust yourself.

Until you do this, you'll never be able to trust others and you'll put what trust you have in people who will hurt you.

3. Be Honest.

With yourself first because it makes it easier to be honest with others. Honesty will cost you and what it returns is worth it. Tell tall tales, lie with the best of them and exaggerate all you want when people know that's what you're doing. The rest of the time, be honest.

4. Respect people's boundaries and limits.

There's a difference between being selfish and being selfless. Realize what this means for you and you'll realize what it means for others.

5. Keep it Simple.

Because it's so much easier that way.

6. Take responsibility for your actions.

When you make a mistake and before anybody else knows the mistake has been made, raise your hand and say loud enough for others to hear you, "That one's mine. I did that." If the people around you are more interested in pointing their fingers at you and distancing themselves from you than helping you clean things up, you're standing around the wrong people. Let them distance themselves. They won't be around you when you succeed, and you will, because you'll have learned how to stand up tall, proud and free by recognizing, owning up to and cleaning up your own mistakes. From this you'll also learn compassion and dignity and how to help others clean up their mistakes, as well. Along with this ...

7. Mistakes are just that; You can reach again.

So learn to stretch when you have to and to recognize when what you're reaching for isn't something you'd want to hold in your hands. You'll be better for it and so will those who love you.

8. Innocence is not Naivety and vice-versa.

Think of this as a self-recognition of " ... wise as serpents and harmless as doves."

9. Your rights end where your willingness to harm and hurt begin.

If you need this one explained or you needed a moment to put this into a context you could get comfortable with, you are either intentionally ignorant (never a good plan) or hoping to excuse yourself for your behavior towards others (also not a good plan)

10. Language is a tool, like Maslow's Hammer.

Some people think everything's a nail. Be neither. This is part 1.

11. Language is a tool, and can be Eliadeian.
Some people are or can become 2nd order thinkers. Be both. This is part 2.

12. Faith is with the heart, but the confession of faith is with the lips.
So until you can say it to at least two others, it ain't true and you and others will know it.

13. Everything is that simple.
As soon as you begin saying things are not quite that simple or that things aren't that easy, you've demonstrated you don't understand the true nature of the problem.

14. Be wary of those who only tell you of their successes.
They do not have a full view of life.

15. It is not easier to get forgiveness than permission.
Attempting to do so demonstrates a lack of concern and consideration for others.

16. Be thee not a respecter of men (or women).
Respect is earned through actions that are closely aligned with words, and both are externalizations of thoughts, beliefs and ideas, which brings us back to what you get when you squeeze an orange.

17. Do not go where you are not invited.
This, in all things, because being unwelcome can be a painful experience in more ways than one, and the corollary is that you'll always find your way to where you're wanted and loved.

18. Do not do what you are not asked to do.
Because until you are asked, you're doing it for yourself, not for them, and it may not be what they wanted in the first place.

19. People who don't ask for what they want deserve what they get.

So go ahead and ask. All a "no" means is that there must be other avenues you haven't explored yet.

20. Never, via your direct action or intentional inaction, allow others to come to harm.

And the minute you begin debating what "harm" is, you've already allowed it to happen.

21. If someone is drowning don't ask them "How wet is the water?"

Make sure your questions are relevant to the situation you are asking about. Think before you speak, otherwise be prepared for those around you to care more about keeping themselves dry than helping you to safety.

22. You are not your brother's (or your sister's) keeper.

Show people enough respect to let them make their own mistakes. That way they'll be able to appreciate their own successes.

23. If you can't think outside the box then you'll spend your life as someone else's package.

And maybe you're comfortable with that. We're not.

24. Don't feed someone when you're hungry.

You'll be jealous of what they eat and there's no guarantee there'll be any left for you when they're done.

25. In the Game of Life, let the other person win once in a while.

You'll learn to be humble, they'll learn to be gracious. At some point in time they'll figure out what you did, then they'll learn to be humble and you'll learn to be gracious.

26. What is a Dark Mystery to you is Perfectly Obvious to someone else (and vice versa).

So when you explain something to somebody, explain the obvious. When you leave something out and they don't get it, you're the fool, not them.

27. Everybody knows there are classes in society, any society.

Wise people don't speak of it. The wisest people don't show it.

28. Respect people who know the name of their waiter or waitress.

It shows they value people.

29. Everything is possible.

When you decide something is impossible all you've done is demonstrate the limitations of your resources.

30. To each of us is given a measure, to some great and to some so small as not to be noticed in the light of day.

How can we know that the greatest measure, without the efforts of those barely noticed as foundation or support or crown, will be enough? Therefore never slight nor be jealous of those whose measure is greater or less than yours, because to each of us is given a measure. It's not the measure that makes us great, it's what we do with our measure that gives us greatness.

31. You don't always need a reason to get something done.

Sometimes things just have to be done, and that is reason enough.

32. Own your history. Don't be owned by it.

You are the only one who has the power to change the universe you live in.

33. Sometimes you just have to let the fool be slapped.

People know when they're not being upfront, honest, above board, ... , and nine times out of ten they want to be caught because it gives shape, form, and substance to the world around them. You honor them and yourself by catching them. Regarding that one out of ten that doesn't want to be caught? Put up walls between yourself and them. They will be a danger to both themselves and to you.

34. Never be afraid to appear a fool when asking a question.

It's the ones who won't ask questions who are truly the fools.

35. Be wary of people who enjoy casting large shadows.

It is better to be the light that allows shadows to exist, that lights the way for others, than to be in someone else's darkness.

36. Courage is not the absence of fear. Courage is what you do when you're afraid.

Be Courageous. It will cost you relationships, no doubt, but you'll be able to sleep at night.

37. When someone is hanging onto a cliff by their fingernails, don't ask them if they want to play catch.

Another example of making sure your questions are relevant to the situation. People in need, people under stress and strain, when distracted, suffer. Make sure you help rather than hurt.

38. Let your dreams create your capabilities.

Never believe that what you are now is all you ever shall be.

39. Some will ask, "What do you want?" Others with, "Who are you?" To answer either, you must first answer "Am I who I want to be?"

Whether known or not, spoken or not, it is the first question that must be answered.

40. Laws are the boundaries societies place upon the spirit.

Be boundless. You may be in a society of one, but being alone is often the price of freedom.

41. Never allow yourself to be blinded by those who lack vision.

Surround yourself with those who encourage you to see, even if they can not. It is much to be preferred than to be around those who won't allow you to see because they themselves can not.

42. Shame is a gift given by someone who fears you.

This can be a hard lesson to learn. The only reason for someone to make you feel ashamed is to control you, and love has no need for control.

43. If you follow your path long enough, eventually you'll discover your dreams.

Therefore it is up to you to make sure your dreams are something you want to discover.

44. and in keeping with the above, Paths reveal themselves to you if you let them.

They are not always straight and often not obvious, therefore it's up to you to follow or not as you decide.

45. Acceptance is not Understanding.

Keep separate the things you accept and the things you understand. A few items will be in both camps, a lot of items won't. Knowing the difference means knowing what you're willing to change versus what you're willing to let change you, and the world of difference is there.

46. As with most things, if you're willing to go just a little bit further than you've ever gone before, an entirely new world

47. is opened onto you.

Explore to the limits of your abilities and willingness. It's the only way to know how big you really are.

48. Is it better to see the end, to hear its answer when you call its name, or to be there?

Answer these and you'll know what eternity means to you.

49. True Authority becomes such by acknowledging, understanding and incorporating all points of view, especially those that disagree.

Authority can not exist without growth and change, and authority that can't include or disprove disagreement is no authority at all.

50. Success is not synonymous with Achievement.

People can have successful careers and have achieved nothing in their life, while people who've achieved but one thing are successful beyond measure. Success means you've grown (no small achievement, that). Achievement means you've helped someone else grow (and to be willing just to take on that task indicates you're a success).

51. "Chaos, once defined, can be the most organized system there is." and "Don't burn your bridges before they hatch." are two orthogonal statements and their intersection is you.

Take the time to realize that these two statements are equations of existence and that they define a universe of possibilities. Recognize that if they intersect you are the intersection and that if they don't intersect you're denying yourself a universe of possibilities.

52. Always be willing to share your story and always be respectful of the stories of others.

Tell people "I will tell you as much of my story as you wish to know, but I will never share your story with others nor will I share another's story with you." Understand this and you'll understand your own and other's boundaries, where you begin and end and how your words can heal and hurt others.

53. If you can't clearly say "No" then nobody will know when you're saying "Yes".

So be clear and concise in all your communications when a "No" or a "Yes" will do. People will appreciate it and confusions will quickly melt away.

54. Handing over control is not giving up responsibility.

Hand over control of something to someone else and they become your responsibility as well as whatever you have control of. Consider this an opportunity to teach, yourself and them.

55. Never let your limitations be someone else's limitations.

You've probably worked long and hard to get the ones you have. Don't share them. Similarly, honor the ones others have that you don't. They worked just as hard to get theirs as you did to get yours.

56. Sometimes the best lesson is recognizing that someone is not your teacher.

It can save both of you a lot of pain and sorrow.

57. Paddle Plato's Life Boat with Ockham's Razor.

Find a theoretical structure that supports all data, even conflicting data, and find a theoretical structure that supports it all without resorting to unnecessary entities. This is where The Principle of Rich Observation meets The Principle of Parsimony. Live there. Be there. Be it.

58. You must be dancing yourself if you want to dance with somebody.

You can not find what you're looking for until and unless you're willing to first be it yourself.

59. Eliminate Variables, Remove Ambiguities.

You are going to make mistakes in life (see Principles 6, 7, and 22). It's possible to minimize those mistakes by eliminating as many unknowns as possible from the situation before you act. You can further minimize mistakes by removing all ambiguous information before you act. It isn't possible to ignore ambiguous information and it's usually possible to act in a way that doesn't require making use of the ambiguous data. Be patient. Ambiguous situations tend to resolve themselves given enough time. How do they resolve? By eliminating unknowns.

60. Be An Enemy of the People, point out the naked Emperor, protect The Old Man and tell people about The Rock.

You may be the only one who knows the truth and in truth, you're the only one who can know your own truth. However, that doesn't make the truth incorrect and your sharing it can possibly save lives. Even if it costs you yours.

61. It is perfectly useless to know the answer to the wrong question.

So before you answer another's question ask yourself if the question is worth answering at all.

62. Never cure a singer of their voice.

Sometimes people's gifts can frighten or disturb us, hence their gifts go unappreciated. Take a moment to make sure your goal is to be just and that your pursuit isn't just for yourself at the expense of others.

63. Choice is better than no choice.

This isn't Free Will versus Predestination, this is right here, right now, do you want to be in control of your life or give up control? The latter leads to victimization and can't be healthy for anyone involved. The former leads to opportunity and possible sacrifice, but it'll be your choice to sacrifice if you do.

64. Don't label people (for both your sakes).
It's sometimes helpful to assign labels to people so long as you remember that people are not objects, labels are like boxes and boxes can become coffins. For both of you.

65. Work honestly, accurately, and unbiasedly.
Doing so will be your testimony. And while some may despise you, the majority will recognize that you honor them through your work and return that honor a hundred-fold.

66. A worker is worthy of their wages.
Recognize that nothing is free. That's first. Somebody is paying some where at some time any time some thing is done. Directly paying the worker for work done demonstrates you value them and their work, that you recognize them as equals in a fair-exchange, and (perhaps most importantly) that you respect yourself enough to know your own value is not in question. That last one throw you? Then go elsewhere. The only time people want something for free is when they're not sure of the value of their own efforts because the price people are willing to pay is a measure of the value they place on their request. Want something for free? Then it has little value to you. Willing to pay? Then it's important to you. It's as simple as that.

The other side of this is that the worker can ask for wages in other than coin of the realm (and barter doesn't count. Barter is mutually agreed to coin of the realm). Recognize that the only commerce besides coin of the realm is with a piece of yourself — your time, your strength, your thoughts, your word, your knowledge, your wisdom, your friendship, your oath. Be careful with these. Coin is far cheaper than heart.

67. Act with kindness even though you don't know the

outcome.

Never doubt that something you said or didn't say, did or didn't do, etc., changed the universe in some incredible way. The Universe's concept of the Butterfly Effect is "You said hello to someone walking down the street whom you didn't know therefore a lifeless planet is starting to form oceans."

68. Until you've gathered all the data available and understood its significance in the situation under study, your decisions regarding the situation are inherently flawed.

Even if they're the correct decisions, the decision process is flawed and outcomes are reproducible due more to luck than knowledge because you never know if the lacking data is contributing 1 or 99% to a complete solution. Explaining observed outcomes without complete knowledge of what's causing them is a fool's goal.

69. Forgive others so that you can be released from their grasp.

Forgiveness isn't done for others, it's done for yourself, to help you let go of the emotions that bind you to someone who wronged you. This does not mean you must love them, only that you may let them go.

70. Faith, until it is tested, is just an opinion.

It doesn't matter if faith takes the form of fealty to a friend, a place, a country, a product, an idea, a life-partner or a deity, until that faith is tested it is just opinion about your relationship to a friend, a place, et cetera. Tested, you know the limits of your faith and limits are just that, neither failure nor triumph, only today's boundaries and limits, only how far you'll go today in this particular test.

71. Technology is not how we make and keep relationships. We make and keep relationships because of who we are, not

what tools we use to stay in touch.

Everybody's lives are hectic. If you can't get everything done you want to do and are missing appointments/meetings/friends/what-have-you, getting more technology won't organize your day because time isn't your problem, you are. You have as much time in your day as Michelangelo, Galileo, Newton, Einstein, Gandhi, Mother Teresa, Buddha, Socrates, …

72. An individual can only receive a certain benefit if others are willing to take on a certain burden.

Remember, the Universe works in balance. From Principles 1, 4, 6, 9, 20, … , remember that what you take you owe. Think you don't often enough, think this doesn't apply to you often enough and you'll find yourself on the long end of burden. Not a happy place.

73. When someone shares their success with you, focus on them, not you. There's no need to compare their success to yours. This is their moment, not yours.

Imagine your toddler or a friend's toddler taking their first step. Would you tell them about your first step? This Principle is a corollary to 14. Help people celebrate their successes. Especially those they struggled for. And earned.

Appendix: Definitions

What Was NextStage?

Long, long ago and in an internet far, far away, there was a little, tiny company with a base, disruptive technology that planted itself in twenty different fields (industries). That little, tiny company took root in nineteen of the twenty.

Not bad for a freakin' farmboy from Nova Scotia, right?

Okay, now seriously ...

From 1995 to 2016 Susan (wife/partner/Princess) and I had a company called *NextStage Evolution* based on a technology I created in our basement (I know it sounds apocryphal and it's true. You can read about it in *Reading Virtual Minds Volume I: Science and History* http://nlb.pub/MindsV1). According to the USPTO (United States Patent and Trade Office - the place you get patents in the US, and these are their words, not ours) "NextStage has created a technology that allows any machine to understand and respond to human thought through any human-machine interface."

Such a technology (in the mid-late 1990s) was *base* - meaning, as one of our early investors said - it was like plastic. We could make a milk bottle out of it, a car dashboard, picnic cutlery, basketballs, anything. It was disruptive because it could change how lots of things were done.

That it did, in many industries and not all.

Eventually the technology - which we called *Evolution Technology* - was in use in some 125 countries. We had offices in four countries and representation in about thirty others.

We could have been even more widespread, and our Principles (in Appendix: Principles) stopped us.

Read through those Principles and you learn a lot about us, the people we hired, the companies we worked with, and what we were willing to do.

And after some twenty years, we needed a break. We started off-loading pieces of *Evolution Technology* to the companies and people we thought would use it wisely and well.

So far, so good.

Shortly after this off-loading process began, Susan said, "I've never seen you happier than when you're writing your stories. We don't have to worry about money anymore, so I want you to write your stories from now on."

Ever obedient, I did and am.

By the way, that "freakin' farmboy from Nova Scotia" line comes from my demonstrating *Evolution Technology* to the then Dean of MIT's Sloan School. At the end of the demonstration, he rolled his eyes and muttered (in front of our then VP), "I have the whole goddamn Media Center down the street from me and some f'ing farmboy from Nova Scotia figures this out?"

I stared at him for a moment and he met my gaze.

"I said that out loud, didn't I?"

"Yep."

Define NextStageologist

I mentioned in *Define NextStage* about people we hired. We hired from all over the globe, all races, all ethnic groups, all genders, all nationalities. There were three things all of them had in common:
1. An unsatiable curiosity
2. Colloquial fluency in two or more languages
3. Lots of life experience (they could be chronologically young so long as they had lots of life experience)

We knew going in we were going to be a different company. All our people were work-on-demand, not employees per se, and we paid them well enough they could afford private insurance, vacations, holidays, and the like. We had a firm three-strikes policy; you could make any one type of mistake twice. A third time with the same kind of mistake and you were out (because you weren't learning). But you could make lots of different kinds of mistakes so long as you learned and grew from them.

We also paid for them to go to school and take any classes they wished, no obligation for repayment and no grade requirements (that's the unsatiable curiosity department). We figured anything you learned would benefit both you and us, even if what you learned was the class or training was worthless to you.

The language fluency requirement dealt with *Evolution Technology* being partially based on language (my patents covered anthropology, linguistics, mathematics, neuroscience, and a bunch of other disciplines. One of our people once counted and came up with 120. Nice grouping, that, and mainly because I borrowed from lots of disciplines rather than reinvent what I needed when someone else already did it. This is called translational research, and is mentioned in some of this book's chapters).

Also regarding language and life experience, we wanted people who knew language is a tool, i.e., if someone's language or what they say upsets you, first recognize what they say has more to do with them than you, and second use your upsetness as a tool to learn more about your own issues rather than being hostile to them and theirs.

And there's probably more.

We're still in touch with many of them, and all were and are our teachers.

Who are yours?

And What Was The NextStage Irregular?

NextStage had clients all over the world, and many of them were researchers themselves (Susan and I come from heavy research backgrounds). Business clients constantly asked if we could get *Evolution Technology* to do certain things and, if the problem intrigued me, Susan et al had a tough time holding me back from solving it. Most times it only involved defining the root elements of the problem, writing the mathematics involved in the root definitions, then teaching ET (that's what we ended up calling *Evolution Technology*) to do the math.

And each time we came up with interesting research or needed people to test a tool developed to solve a client problem, we let people know via our newsletter, *The NextStage Irregular*, so called because we were NextStage and we never sent it out at regular intervals.

Hey, it was our sandbox, we could play in it the way we liked.

Curious about Joseph's fiction?

Here are excerpts from three *Tales Told Round Celestial Campfires* stories. Enjoy!

Cymodoce

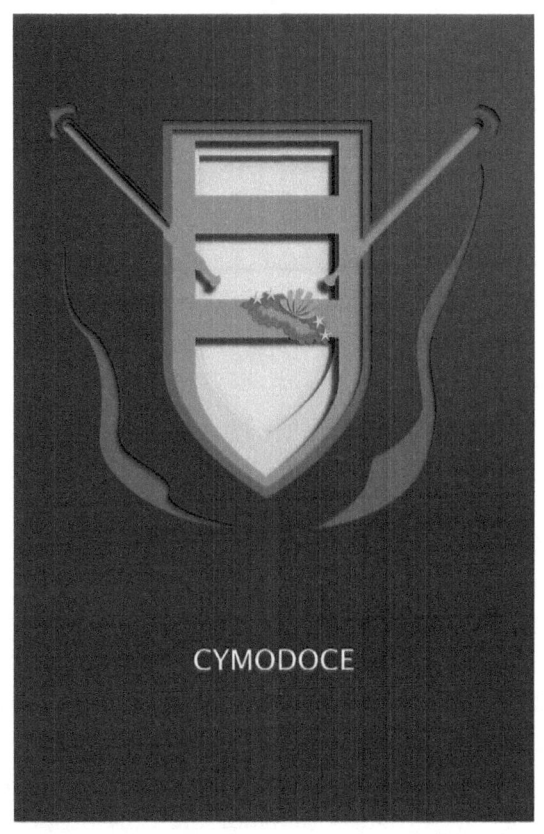

*"How happy could I be with either
Were t'other dear charmer away!
But while ye thus tease me together,
To neither a word will I say."*

Synopsis

Jenny Packwood, a single mother of three-year-old twins Davy and Cymmi and ASL interpreter/teacher in New York City, returns to her family's Maine Coast cabin for a summer away. There she remembers the near-dead man she found on the beach whom she nursed back to health.

Her kindness and his tenderness resulted in a night's quiet passion. He was gone when she woke, taking nothing nor using her skiff to get to shore.

He never returned.

Now back on the island with the children from their one encounter, Jenny finds seashell necklaces and deep-water pearls - gifts similar to her lover's previous visit - on her dock, in her boat, and on the path up to her cabin.

One night he returns. He knows the children are his.

And he wants one to come with him.

Excerpt

Jenny silently guided the rowboat to the dock, all the while keeping one eye on her three-year-old twins, Davy and Cymmi, sitting in front of her. When the boat was next to the mooring Jenny grabbed a line, pulled the boat to the dock and tied it. It was the first time she'd been to the island since the twins were born. Her parents, who died within a week of each other the previous fall, left her the dock, the boat, the cabin, the two acres of land, and only property taxes and upkeep to concern her.

Davy fidgeted. "Mommy, I'm hungry. Can we eat now?" She put a finger to her lips and Davy pouted. Cymmi was leaning over the side of the boat, splashing her hands in the water. She paused, looked out over the waves, then splashed harder.

Jenny moored the boat, lifted a lunch basket and helped the children onto the dock. "Mom," Davy whined, "I'm hungry."

"We'll go up to the cabin and eat. Okay, Davy?" They started up the narrow path.

"Mom, Cymmi's still by the water."

Jenny looked up. Cymmi was in up to her ankles. Jenny dropped the lunch basket, ran back and lifted Cymmi from the water. Her feet glistened. Cymmi kept looking at the waves as Jenny sat her by the lunch basket, took out a container of fresh water and poured it over Cymmi's feet. The tiny, silvery marks began to fade and Jenny signed /COME /EAT /NOW /PLAY /LATER /OKAY/?// She took Cymmi's hand and gently pulled her along.

Much later, when Jenny had put the children to bed, she walked down the path and sat on the dock. She took off her sandals and swished her feet in the ocean. Across the Sound she could see the lights of the Maine coast. The island had always been a quiet place. Even in the heat of the tourist season, when Route 1, heard if not seen across the Sound, was a tangle of campers, buses, and hitchhikers, the island was left to the three New York families who owned it and had cabins there.

The sounds of summer came across the water. She tried to match the sounds with the lights. Fuzzy rock music came from Beniroo's, an old icehouse turned bar and nightclub. When Beniroo's music paused she could hear a calliope and, intermittently, people giddily screaming. That would be Funland. She could see the Ferris wheel spinning and the roller coaster trestle climbing into the sky. Search lights swept back and forth, sweeping the ocean mists inland and then back out to sea. To the north she could pick out the tinny guitar and muffled bass of The Word's tent meeting, preaching God's message to the summer sinners.

Something tickled her foot and she jerked it from the water. Soon the tide would turn and go out. Fundy had powerful tides, aided this night by the moon overhead. There was a splash out by the rocks. Something bobbed briefly about forty feet from her. She heard another splash, saw a rippling approach her through the waves. /HELLO/?//

"Mommy?" Davy's voice pulled her back to dry land.

There was a slight almost soundless splash in the water.

Jenny's heart pounded. She fumbled getting up. "Yes, Davy?"

He walked over to her. "Who're you talking to?"

She smiled and ruffled his hair. "Just the fishes. I told them we came back this summer. Now, what are you doing out of bed?"

"I couldn't sleep."

She lifted him up so he could ride her hip as she walked. He wrapped his arms around her neck and cradled his head in her shoulder. "Come on, little man, you can sleep with me tonight." Davy's arms hung limp by his sides before they got back to the cabin.

She put Davy in her own bed and checked Cymmi before returning to the kitchen. There she made herself a cup of coffee and, from a window, watched the coast lights go out, one by one.

The Goatmen of Aguirra

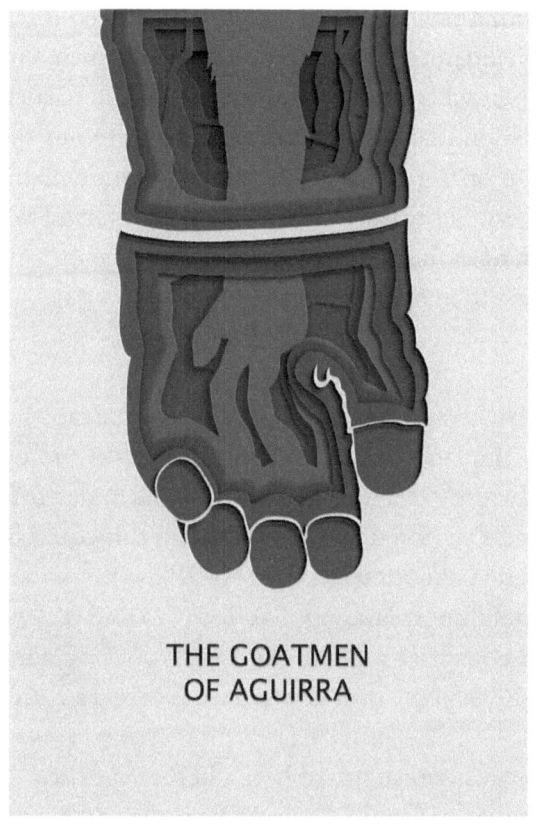

"If you live knowing only a process, you can never have all your options. If you live knowing there are options, one of them can be to partake in the process, they tell me."

Synopsis

Leaving behind his estranged wife and son, xenopologist Gordon Banks sets out with an advance team on a mission to explore the distant planet Aguirra. There, the team discovers the Goatmen: wise aboriginals with a rich telekinetic history preserved through entheogenic ritual. Nicknamed "Journeyer" by the Goatmen, Gordon Banks is invited to their village to live amongst them and participate in their customs. He soon realizes that the Goatmen are not the only intelligent life form on Aguirra and - in the process - embarks on a path of self-discovery. Set against the backdrop of interstellar colonialism, The Goatmen of Aguirra proposes that one's destiny can be achieved on a path taken to avoid it.

Excerpt

705015:216 - We've landed in a grotto, near the center of Hochebene's Altiplano, but closer to the Towers of God than not. On one side of the grotto is the only run of clear water for some thirty kilometers, and I've noted with Sanders that this could be a problem as all native fauna encountered thus far follow the same biologies as we. Immediately upon landing, Sanders ordered Tellweiller, Nash, and Galen to construct a blind. We are now a boulder, one among several, that slid into the grotto when we lowered a rumbler to cover our landing.

Nash estimates two standard hours before sunrise.

Early estimates indicated Aguirra was three and a half to four billion years old. Now, with readings coming in about the deep core and mantle, we place it closer to five. Gravity is one-point-one standard and the atmosphere is quite like Earth's only sweeter due to a higher O3 content. There is also a free floating enzyme, essentially carbolic anhydrase, which explains some of the evolutionary adaptations on the planet. Everything we've observed is based on the nitrocarbon cycle – everything we've recorded from space and robotics shows up as a variation on some earth fauna – and the carbolic anhydrase probably helps redaction and reduction in the O3 rich atmosphere when a stressing agent is introduced.

Due to the atmosphere there is a perpetual slight pink tint in the sky, much like before an intense electrical storm back home. This area, Hochebene's Altiplano to the Towers of God, is a paragneiss formed we're not sure how long ago by glaciation. It is difficult to estimate because the atmosphere mediates the planetary temperature such that weathering is neither gradual nor minimal – Hopkin's Bioclimatic Law doesn't seem to apply. There are seasons in the temperate zones but without the fluctuations of four true seasons. Summer temperature extremes range from -19°C to 33°C. Winter temperatures also vary by about twenty degrees, from -25°C to 5°C. These temperatures are for our current location, 43°N, 8000m altitude, and, as I've mentioned earlier, shrouded to the west by the Towers of God.

To our immediate east is the rock wall we worked hard to resemble, the rise of the grotto, then the expanse of the high plain for several kilometers. Although comprised principally of paragneiss and granite with only slight eruptions of soil, a hardy tundral grass grows in clumps all around. Our guess is the grass serves to anchor what little soil there is in place. There are wind storms – one is due in another hour – when Astarte 217 rises over the altiplano and begins churning this high, thin air with the thicker, deep valley air far below.

These grasses are richly verdant, their tops a slight yellow as if gently burned. Galen collected some samples when the blind was completed and says the yellowing is a pollen. Thus we learn immediately that these verdant clusters aren't true grasses and that there is some pollenizing agent, perhaps only the wind, which is at work. If the robotics sent into these highlands hadn't met such abrupt and catastrophic ends, we might know more about Aguirra's highland life, at least in this area.

There is still a carpet of snow, albeit thin and frayed in some areas, stretching a kilometer from the entrance to the altiplano to the Towers of God even though this continent is now in high summer. The snow, Nash says, is due to the altitude and rarified atmosphere. Even with the carpet of white, this is a desert, with cold, dry steppes leading to the Towers.

In contrast to earth flora, there appears to be no treeline. While there are no trees on the altiplano, there are five here in the grotto ranging from two to two-fifty meters in height. They appear something like succulent scotch pines, kind of chubby Christmas trees. They have no root systems and, according to Galen, all five trees are extensions of the same growth and are more like vines than trees, growing like Sequoias in the northern California forests. If they are vines, it explains their limbs being naked on one side and holding fast against the grotto's walls. They're being succulents so close to a clear water supply indicates that the water might be seasonal.

There are several similar although much smaller trees, these resembling elms and birch although Galen's report might show different, growing to our west and in the runoff fissures of the Towers. From there these trees grow up to the crowns of the Towers, becoming deeper and denser with altitude, giving the appearance of twin green-haired giants out in the distance. Based on this and other evidence Galen claims these are not true "trees". If Galen's contention about the succulents is accurate, there are but one or two of these "trees" sending their shoots, binding and girding like some giant's phylacteries, up the Towers.

The most noticeable feature of the landscape, the one we all knew would be most breath-

taking, are the Towers themselves. We are eight kilometers above sea level and the Towers rise another eight above us. They are the largest vertical features on all of Aguirra, even and symmetrical in every geologic detail, with their expansive flat plained plateau heads, each five-point-five kilometers in diameter, separated by zero-point-five kilometers horizontal and a four kilometer drop. There are a few passes down the Towers, more like torrents than actual passes in their slope and grain, and various hanging, piedmont, and steppe glaciers coming down the Towers' sides. The best climb, if one were necessary, seems to be along a bergschrund on the immediate faces of each.

Tellweiller has no explanation for the Towers' formation, although it is obvious from their age they were formed in the prebiologic days of the planet.

Although I am not a religious man, standing at their feet and hearing the winds, it is not difficult to imagine the whispers the ancient Greeks heard about Mt. Olympus. I can understand why these features were named the Towers of God.

Mani He

MANI HE

"The more you accept your fear, the greater your courage will become."
"Some places, they'll be like nightmares. Other places, they'll be like your sweetest dreams. Go towards your sweetest dreams, Mani He."

Synopsis

Anthony Morelli is on the fast track becoming Boston's next high-finance wunderkind. But his ascendency has an unforeseen cost; a soon-to-retire workmate is fired to make room for him. His organization's CEO only wants a "man's man" in the role and tells Anthony to prove himself via a solo trip to the organization's northern New Hampshire hunting cabin for a weekend.

Just be sure to bring home a trophy to hang in his office.

But Anthony was raised to respect The Wild. His Native American grandfather told him stories about the animal spirits, told Tony The Old Ones were his friends. Now Tony's childhood beliefs want his ascending star to travel another sky.

Anthony agrees to the trip and what Tony learns changes him forever.

Excerpt

Anthony Morelli saw the badger across the street as he came out of South Station, where the MBTA's southern terminus washed people towards One Financial Place. Anthony wore his St. James suit – bright grays with a black pinstripe – with cream oxford shirt and red and gold pumped satin tie, diamond studs, stockings which blended with his trousers, and black wingtips. It was an early Boston Fall and Channel-4 forecasted light drizzle. Morelli's raincoat was draped over his left arm and his accountant's case pulled down his right like a ship's keel in a storm. Today he made the presentation showing the errors in Thompson's plan.

The badger sat on a pretzel wagon. People were buying soft pretzels with mustard, soft pretzels with cheese, soft pretzels with extra salt. The badger was passing small talk and change and nobody else seemed to notice.

Morelli stopped and stared. The smell of coal-cooked chestnuts, peanuts and pretzels came over the diesel and street-level smog of Boston. His mouth watered and he remembered his father teaching him how to flip peanuts and catch them in his mouth.

The badger looked at Tony and hollered, "REDhots! PRETzels! GETcha-GETcha REDhots! PRETzels!"

If Anthony wore his glasses, he'd've adjusted them. Today he wore his contacts but his hands went to his face anyway. The badger waved at him and laughed, mimicking Tony's hand movements. The badger started pedaling his pretzel wagon and rolled away, calling out "REDhots! GETcha REDhots!"

Tony went into One Financial Place, made his presentation, shook hands, got his back patted, and was thanked personally by the Old Man. Brumhall, the Old Man, looked fifty and was well past seventy-five. His eyes were clear and sharp and his mind had never dulled. Haggedorn, Brumhall's number two, stopped Tony outside Thompson's door. "Anthony, excellent! You planned this? Excellent. Impressed me, right here," Haggedorn tapped his heart. "The Old Man and I gotta talk. It'll be excellent. Thompson. Have to let him go. Too bad. It'll be excellent."

Just then Thompson opened his door, stared at the two men, excused himself, and walked towards the restroom.

Tony looked at Thompson, the way the man's shoulders sagged, the way his chin quivered. Tony swallowed and felt a lump like a badger claw etch its way down his throat, crashing into his stomach like a bus into a pushcart. He wanted to say releasing Thompson wasn't part of his plan. Instead he dug into his pocket for the roll of TUMS his wife, Grace, gave him when he left the house, popped one in his mouth, and made a note to pick up a fresh roll when he went for lunch.

The Old Man came up to them a few moments after Thompson returned to his office. "Mr. Morelli, take the afternoon off. You come in tomorrow, you stop here." Brumhall pointed at Thompson's door and nodded to his number two, acting as if Tony no longer existed. "Mr. Haggedorn." The Old Man opened Thompson's door without knocking.

Haggedorn nodded. Before entering Thompson's office and while the door was opened, he said, "The American Express office. Third

Floor. Our branch, right there. Excellent. Stop in there. Big surprise. It'll be excellent."

Tony said, "I need to get my things."

Haggedorn said, "Already taken care of. Third Floor. American Express. Excellent," and closed Thompson's door.

Tony, still stunned and feeling hollow, took the stairs.

There was a Platinum Plus card with the company name on it waiting for him on the third floor. He smiled, lifted the card to his nose and inhaled like it was a roll of bills and he was an old-time gambler. Another whiff and the smell of platinum plastic rubbed the sting of Thompson's misfortune away. "Excellent." He sniffed the card again.

He took a cab home. From the Financial District to dying but ethnic Revere, even though his mail went thirty miles away to a PO box in affluent and upscale Newton. As the cab went through the Callahan Tunnel the lights went out. The cab starting bucking and kicking, as if the gas and brake had suddenly become alien to the burnt-ash-black West Somalian cab driver. The cab started to weave and horns blared in front, in back, and to the sides of them. Tony leaned forward and tapped on the glass. The burnt-ash-black man looked over his shoulder and Tony slumped back into his seat.

The West Somalian driver was a moose, the driver's dreadlocks weaving through the moose's antlers. He bellowed apologetically in the driver's pidgin English, "Sorry. In my country, we have nothing like this."

Outside his home, Tony gave the West Somalian moose a fifty dollar tip. The moose lifted the bill to his nose much as Tony had done with the Platinum card, inhaled, kissed the bill, then inhaled again. He smiled at Tony and Tony thought he said "Ganja." Tony couldn't be sure because there were grasses and weeds dripping from the driver's mouth. He pulled a U-ey, waved at Tony and left.

Tony waved until Grace called him inside. "Why're you home? Are you okay? You didn't get fired, did you?"

He explained. They celebrated. Later, they went to a quiet little bistro back in the North End, a place they knew from childhood, a place where they were part of the family. They spent the day sipping espressos and talking their first generation Italian-American English with Danté, the owner and the man who introduced them. Tony jumped up from his chair and hurried Grace into her coat when Danté brought some antipasto and linguine pesto.

"Anthony, what's wrong?" asked Grace.

"Nothing. I … I don't feel good. Too much strain. I have to go home."

A long, thin, pink tongue snapped out of a lizard's face atop Danté's body. "Antonio, stai male?" The lizard said.

Tony's face blanched and he wouldn't look the lizard in the eye. The lizard grabbed the water pitcher and a bowl from an empty table. He put the bowl down in front of Tony and poured some water in it, then sprinkled some olive oil on top of the water and placed the salt shaker beside the bowl. He made the sign of the evil eye and motioned Tony to pick up the salt. "Malocchio." The lizard stared fixedly at the bowl of water and oil, waiting for Tony to finish the evil eye ceremony.

At hearing the intervention against misfortune, Tony looked up again. Danté was once again old Danté, the man they'd both known since childhood. The scaly lizard's face and great round eyes, seen for a moment, were gone. His tongue was hidden in his mouth and not whipping about casting for flies as it had been a moment before.

Not believing in the old ways but honoring his friend, Tony sprinkled some salt in his hand, pressed it to his forehead, made the sign of the Cross with his thumb against his forehead and dipped the thumb into the oily water. The oil separated, fleeing from the salt as it lowered the specific gravity of the water. Tony knew the science but couldn't bring himself to shatter the old man's faith. "Si, amico mio. Si."

Late that night, Tony and Grace lay in bed. "It sounds like you've been working too hard, Tony. I don't mind being rich, but I don't want to be rich alone." She rolled on top of him and straddled him. "You die, Mister, and I'll have somebody else in this bed before your breath is cold."

It was an old joke. They both laughed. Up against the wall on the other side of the room and in a line of sight behind Grace's head, a spider built a web above Tony's closet. Tony's eyes focused and zoomed on the spider as if they were camera lenses. Grace was still laughing and rocking on his hips. He saw the spider look up from her web building, hold a pedipalp in front of her eyes and shake it like a finger, shaking her head, "no", as if in warning.

Then the spider was just a simple spider, building a web. Tony's last thought as he went to sleep was, "How did I know it was a 'she'?"

He woke up before the alarm went off. It was daylight and he saw by the clock he had about ten minutes of sleep left. He rolled over, towards his dresser and away from his wife. The badger was picking through the things on his dresser.

It looked up at him and said, "You got any juju-bees?"

Tony shook his head, no.

"How about toys, you got any toys? Coyote likes toys. That dumb shit's always playing with toys."

Another voice called from the hallway. The voice echoed and Tony knew it was coming from the pulldown stairs that led to the attic. "Found 'em." He heard something bumping up in the rafters then the same voice squealed, "Hey, look at this! Tonkas! The kid's got Tonkas!"

The alarm brizzed over Tony's head and Badger said, "See you later, kid. Gotta go."

Grace swacked the alarm silent and said, "Wake up, hon. Time to make me a millionaire."

Tony opened his eyes and reached on his dresser for his glasses. They weren't were he left them the night before. They were shifted a few inches to the right. A coldness shivered him despite the warmth of the bed. On his way to the bathroom he saw the attic stairs bolted and secured in the ceiling and laughed at himself. "Probably got up last night and moved my glasses myself," he mumbled.

In the bathroom he started the shower, turned to the toilet and fell backwards into the tub when he lifted the seat.

Grace called from the bedroom, "You okay, hon?"

"Yeah. Yeah, sure. Just slipped." He turned the shower to cold and held his head under the blast of frigid water. "Okay. I'm awake," he whispered. Drops of cold water trickled down his face, chest and shoulders as he looked back in the toilet. A child's bow and arrow were wedged in the seat.

His old bow and arrow. The bow and arrow which he'd packed under the Tonkas in his toy chest in the attic. The old bow and arrow his grandfather had given him. Holding them he remembered his grandfather's smell, a laborer's smell, his grandfather strong like a farmer. "My people use to be warriors," he once told Tony. "That was long before I met your grandmother." He remembered going to meet other old men with his grandfather, other old men who wore the strange turquoise and silver, bone and bead jewelry his grandfather wore. Then, too soon it seemed, Grandfather John died and the bow and arrow, the old men with the funny jewelry, were no more.

The arrow was rubber tipped and the rubber suction cup was old and cracked. The plastic feathers were stripped in places. The bow was also plastic, with a string made of heavy thread. Feathers and thunderbirds and Indians on horses were painted on the bow. He picked them up and memories of playing Indian as a child came back, as if the memories were waiting like mountain lions in the bow and arrow, waiting to pounce as soon as he touched it.

He lifted the bow and arrow to his shoulder and took aim, hearing himself and others chanting childhood rhymes and verse, mixes of broken English and Hollywood Indians, as he swept the bow and arrow around the bathroom, his arms somehow tiny once again so the toys became big and real and he wasn't Tony Morelli anymore but Little Chief White Feather once again.

He stopped smiling when he took aim at himself in the bathroom mirror. Behind his reflection, a mountain lion pulled back the shower curtain, held out a paw and pointed at the sink. "You wanna hand me the soap there, buddy?"

Tony skipped breakfast and went to work. Haggedorn met him as he got off the elevator at the eighteenth floor. "Anthony. Excellent. New office. Right here. It's yours. It's excellent." It was Thompson's office. A corner office. Two walls of floor-to-ceiling tinted windows with blinds tied to the environmental system. All Anthony had to do was set the amount of light and heat he wanted and the blinds would open and close to accommodate. When necessary, lights and ventilators took up the slack. The name plate on the door – his door, his name. Excellent! – was gold, as was the one on his desk, which was huge. The desk was as big as his bed and the office – his office. Excellent! – was the size of his living room. Along one wall was a multiplexing entertainment system and, at the press of a button, a bar which could rotate from fully alcoholic to totally dry, depending on who you were trying to impress. The other wall had a full length black brocade leather couch. The walls were dark oak, matching the desk. The upholstery of both Tony's chair and the two opposite his desk matched the couch's black. The rug, an inch-thick plush, was gray. He had two computers on his desk and a twenty-channel phone system. The phone's listings were all the ones he'd had in his old office. His accountant's case was there. Along the walls were plants and floral arrangements from various people in the firm and clients he didn't know he had.

As Haggedorn left, the office procession began. Several people came through, all shaking his hand and congratulating him. He looked into their faces as they came and left; this one was too hungry, this one would wait. This one would ally with whoever offered the most, this one would remain loyal.

He stayed late, enjoying the feel of a vibrating, reclining, twelve axes of movement, heated chair and kicked his legs up onto an oak desk so thick it would take six strong men to lift. Somebody knocked on his door. "Yes?"

"Cleaning crew, Mr. Morelli."

Tony checked his watch, a gift from Grace from their dating days when wishes were horses and the two of them rode. "Come on in.

You guys don't waste any time, do you? Office has only been closed about an hour."

The door opened and a hawk pushed a cleaning cart into the room. A hummingbird followed in behind the hawk. Both were dressed in clean and neatly pressed "Ace Cleaning Services" uniforms. The hawk's uniform had a white name tag over the right breast pocket which held an Ace Cleaning Services pocket-protector filled with pencils. Stitched in red was "Sparky". The hummingbird was obviously new because he had no pencils and his name was a red-on-white iron-on tag and not stitched in, therefore showing no permanence. He was "Bob". The hummingbird wore earbuds and hummed a tune Tony couldn't place.

"We try not to waste any time, Mr. Morelli," said Sparky the Hawk. "Sometimes, though, people keep us waiting their whole life."

Hummingbird Bob nodded, "Yeah."

They took out spray bottles and stain removers and went to work.

Haggedorn came in with the Old Man. He looked around the office, told Sparky the Hawk and Hummingbird Bob they were doing a good job and he appreciated their consistency as if there was nothing strange about them, then faced Tony. "You like it here, Mr. Morelli?" asked Brumhall. "This office satisfy you?"

"Yes, sir, thank you. And please call me 'Tony'."

Brumhall nodded slowly, measuring Tony with some internal gauge. "May I see your watch then, Tony?"

"Beg pardon, sir?"

"Your watch."

Tony peeled it from his wrist. Brumhall inspected it. "This watch have any significance to you?"

Tony, his eyes on the watch, swallowed. "No."

"Good." Brumhall tossed the watch into the trash basket on Sparky the Hawk's cart and turned back to Tony. "Mr. Haggedorn."

Tony watched Haggedorn open a black case. Out of the corner of his eye he watched Sparky the Hawk grab Hummingbird Bob's hands as the latter dove for Tony's old watch. Brumhall said nothing until Haggedorn gave Tony the black case.

A new watch. Rivier platinum, with more dials and gauges than Tony imagined he'd find in a fighter cockpit. The back had his name, the date, and "Welcome to The Club."

"You play tennis, Tony?" Brumhall asked.

"No, sir."

Brumhall brow creased. "No? What about Racquetball?"

"No, sir, not that either."

Brumhall turned briefly to Haggedorn then back to Tony. "Golf?"

Tony was about to answer in the negative when Haggedorn interrupted, his voice slightly higher and his face a little whiter than usual, "Outdoorsman. And excellent, Mr. Brumhall. Our Tony. Gun in hand. Right, Tony?"

Before Tony could answer, Haggedorn continued. "Hiking. Camping. Being alone. One man against nature. The outdoor thing. And excellent."

Brumhall considered this for a moment. "You like to hunt?"

Behind Brumhall, Haggedorn stared into Tony's eyes and nodded vigorously. Tony answered, "Yeah."

Hummingbird Bob dropped his spray bottle into the bar's sink. "Sorry."

Brumhall stared at Bob for a second then said, "The company's got a cabin up in New Hampshire." His looked back at Tony, "Did you know that?"

"No sir."

"Is it hunting season, Haggedorn? Is there something he can go up there and kill?"

"Yes, Mr. Brumhall. Something. Something excellent."

"Good. Give him the keys, Haggedorn. Call ahead and make sure he's got provisions for three days. I'll see you on Monday, Mr. Morelli. I'd like to see something strapped to the hood of your car when you come back. Am I understood?" The Old Man's eyes were clear crystals bearing into Tony's face.

"Yes, sir. I think so."

"Good."

Coming Soon From Northern Lights Publishing

Stay up on early reads, special offers, and gift opportunities! Join our mailing list at http://nlb.pub/nlbmailings

June 2023: The Inheritors
Tommy was told he was different by his family, his friends, and his teachers. He was special. Then one day he disappeared, prompting a mystery that would span millennia and bring together individuals from all walks of life from the distant past to the near future. Reaching out across all the world's civilizations through all time, The Inheritors tells the story of the hidden costs of immortality, the innocent lives exploited in its pursuit, and the unlikely heroes who make the ultimate sacrifice to exact justice.

September 2023: The Shaman
Gio Fortuna, a boy spurned by his parents for being "slow," is raised by his grandfather in the ways of the Practice, a rich esoteric discipline drawing upon mystic traditions passed down over thousands

of years from a multitude of cultures. Written in five parts chronicling Gio's life, The Shaman sees Fortuna embark on a journey from initiate to adept, young boy to old man, as he navigates a network of teachers, each with their own unique lessons and challenges. Steeped in wisdom applicable to all, The Shaman is an inspiring story that proposes a unique path to self-discovery and growth unlike anything written before.

December 2023: Search

Two young boys and their guardian go missing in the Maine woods. No one has a clue, no one comes forward offering information, and the police are powerless to provide the boys' family with any answers. The boys' older sister learns about Gio Fortuna through a friend and asks him to help. Search chronicles one life-changing event in The Shaman's life, an event causing Gio to realize the use of his grandfather's teachings and their purpose in both his life and the lives of others.

About Northern Lights Publishing

Northern Lights Publishing/Press is an association of five professionals (one graphic artist, one marketer, one editor/book designer, one copyeditor, one editor/educator/author) and a rotating group of ten published authors and poets all of whom are passionate readers. Financial backing is provided by a small group of investors led by Susan and Joseph Carrabis through the NextStage Evolution Corporation. Everyone receives remuneration and owns an equal share of the company with the exception of Susan and Joseph Carrabis.

We're developing our publishing/marketing model so we're not accepting submissions at present.

We'll open our doors to submissions (and announce it through various social networks) once we're sure we can break even and preferably turn a profit. Until then, wish us well.

It's an exciting journey and one we'd love to share, but only after we're sure we can successfully navigate the publishing seas.

Also by Joseph Carrabis

(Joseph's fiction and non-fiction make great use of the concepts and technologies mentioned in *That Th!nk You Do*)

Non-Fiction

Reading Virtual Minds Volume I: Science and History - http://nlb.pub/Minds1

The science and history behind NextStage Evolution's Evolution Technology

Reading Virtual Minds Volume II: Experience and Expectation - http://nlb.pub/Minds2

Learnings and Take-Aways from NextStage Evolution's research and studies

Reading Virtual Minds Volume III: Fair-Exchange and Social Networks - http://nlb.pub/Minds3

Learnings and Take-Aways from NextStage Evolution's research and studies applied specifically on on- and off-line social interactions

Fiction: Novels

Empty Sky - http://nlb.pub/EmptySky

What if you're a young boy, Jamie McPherson, whose mother has been missing for over a year and whose father starts falling in and out of coma? What if you hold onto your aging dog, Shem, who's always been with you and always protected you, because the world isn't safe anymore?

And what if in the midst all that's happening, The Moon asks you to help her save the world's dreams?

Earl Pangiosi's greatest desire, since childhood, has been to control and manipulate people. Working for the NSA, Earl learns that people's dreams - their nonconscious minds - guide their conscious decisions. Control their dreams - weaponize them - and you control people at an unprecedented level.

Jamie will not face Pangiosi alone. The Moon sends her Guardians, winged, shapeshifting wolves; and her children, The Oneiroi, little black silhouettes, shadows in the darkness of night, whose multicolored, multifaceted, crystalline eyes serve as kaleidoscopic Gates — little rainbow bridges allowing humans passage from one dream reality to the next, to help Jamie.

Pangiosi sends the Native American giant, Nighthorse, to stop Jamie. But Nighthorse's grandfather introduced him to Wovoka, the DreamWorld, as a child. Going after Jamie, Nighthorse finds one of the Oneiroi's Eye-Gates and realizes his grandfather may not have been such a fool after all.

Meanwhile the Moon brings together a team of "Dreamers" to help Jamie. One such Dreamer is ANN, a supercomputer who can blend dream and waking realities via Penrose Consciousnesses, quantum superpositions.

If they fail, Pangiosi and the NSA will control the world.

The Augmented Man - http://nlb.pub/Augmented

Also by Joseph Carrabis

What do you do with a deadly weapon when it's no longer needed?

Nicholas Trailer is the last of The Augmented Men, beings created first by society and completed by a political group the public can't even imagine exists. Captain James Donaldson takes severely abused and traumatized children and modifies them into monsters capable of the most horrifying deeds without feeling any remorse or regret.

But the horrors of war never stay on the battlefield. They always come home.

Battling what society and science has made him, Nick Trailer discovers he is loved. From the horrors of childhood to the horrors of a war, what does it take for someone to find true love and peace? Especially when everyone has their own agenda, from the senators who sanctioned his making to the Governor of Maine who wants to use Nick's struggle to propel himself to the White House.

The Augmented Men were good at war, perhaps a little too good. Now they have to come home ... or do they? What do you do with man-made monsters?

Nick must decide if his friends are his friends and if his enemies are his enemies, all while protecting the woman he loves.

And are you truly the last of your kind?

What if you must remain a monster to defeat a monster? Will you sacrifice love to protect what you love?

Fiction: Anthologies

Tales Told 'Round Celestial Campfires - http://nlb.pub/TalesV1
Includes:

Binky (available separately at http://nlb.pub/Binky)

What if you run an inner-city health clinic and are tired of fighting budget cuts, politics, protestors, police, ... ? And what if you question your purpose because caring is no longer cost-effective? And what if you meet a bright, beautiful child who leads you to a child who died sixty years ago? And what if that child asks you to save its life?

The Boy Who Loved Horses (available separately at http://nlb.pub/

Horses)

What if you're born and raised Hill but got City educated and now you drivin a big state issue Buick back into Hill 'cause you gonna show them you something else? And what if one town you drive through's got secrets it don't want nobody to know? And what if you plan to tell City those secrets and those secrets got they own idea who you gonna tell?

Canis Major (available separately at http://nlb.pub/CanisMajor)

What if you're a WereMan, human when the moon is full, a beast when not, and your father died before explaining your gift to you? And what if your fully human mother did the best she could but couldn't really understand your needs? And what if you're tired of being alone and afraid and once, just once, you want to hold someone and not be afraid of their fear?

Cold War (available separately at http://nlb.pub/ColdWar)

What if your last deployment left you so damaged driving a school bus tops your employable skills? And what if the kids laugh at you because you can't talk right and twitch at nothing? And what if the military calls you back, says they can make you a man again. Or get close. And what if you're so lonely, angry and tired you say sure without realizing they plan to leave you out in the cold, forever?

Cymodoce (available separately at http://nlb.pub/Cymodoce)

What if the only man you've ever given yourself to isn't a man at all? And what if you gave birth to twins, the son wholly yours, the daughter wholly his? And what if your daughter needs to return to her father in order to survive? And what if her survival means never seeing her again, and her brother losing his sister forever?

Dancers in the Eye of Chronos (available separately at http://nlb.pub/Dancers)

What if your love so delights the Gods they grant you immortality.

But you learn love is meant to age, to mature, to grow and change in ways the Gods can't imagine. After millennia, they strip their gift from you. But that's what you wanted; to hold your lover's face one last time before darkness falls. Or is your love so strong it outlives the Gods themselves?

The Goatmen of Aguirra (available separately at http://nlb.pub/Goatmen)
What if you've signed onto a deep space mission and left behind a wife and young son? And what if your mission takes to you a supposedly uninhabited planet that harbors intelligent life that values family above all else? And what if they take you into their family to heal you? And what if, finally healed, your shipmates abandon you when the mission is called home?

Mani He (available separately at http://nlb.pub/ManiHe)
What if you've acquired your dream job but destroyed another man's life and career to get it? And what if the president of your company hands you a rifle and the keys to his mountain cabin with the instructions "Bring me back something to make me proud"? And what if the spirits in the mountains have their own ideas of what it means to be proud?

Power Unlimited (available separately at http://nlb.pub/PowerUnlimited)
What if Eddie's kid brother Tommy idolizes you guys at the gym and wants to be like you but you know he's not really built for it. And what if he sends away for some "GET BIG FAST" Muscle Pill exercise programs? And what if he starts looking like The Hulk and King Kong had a baby? And what if the people who make those Pills want them back?

Sema (available separately at http://nlb.pub/Sema)
What if a beautiful woman discovers you and your friends are

beings living side-by-side with humans since the beginning of time? And what if she discovers you have abilities beyond imagination and she, too, has gifts no mortal should possess? And what if, having no knowledge of your kind, has trained with a Darkness humans can't imagine, never suspecting a Light beyond mortals' dreams?

The Settlement (available separately at http://nlb.pub/Settlement)
What if you're a young, hotshot, wildly successful asteroid miner who hasn't seen your parents since you joined the corp underage? And what if your parents are getting divorced and each is laying claim to guardianship of your fortune? And what if your parents never knew why you joined the corp or what you had to give up to get a ship of your own?

Them Doore Girls (available separately at http://nlb.pub/Doore)
What if the woman you love is the mistress of something else, something so monstrous, so hideous its summoning her creates ocean storms? And what if she knows this entity will destroy her, you, your village and all those you know if she denies it? And what if you know she goes to it willingly because it threatened to kill you, her one love, if she doesn't yield to its wishes?

Those Wings Which Tire, They Have Upheld Me (available separately at http://nlb.pub/Wings)
What if you're a little boy with brain cancer whose doctors say they can cure you by replacing your eyes with an experimental device? And what if that experimental device lets you see your guardian angel? And what if seeing your guardian angel makes you best friends with the class trouble-maker? And what if the class bully finds out you talk to angels?

The Weight (available separately at http://nlb.pub/Weight)
What if you've been a success at everything you've done in your life and decide to retrace a hike you took when wishes were horses

and beggars could ride? And what if you met one of your heroes on that long ago hike and - miracle of miracles - you meet him again? And what if your hero isn't your hero and says you took something from it way back when and now it wants it back?

Winter Winds (available separately at http://nlb.pub/Winds)

What if you're sitting in your favorite chair, your son on your lap, helping him with his homework when you see something in the fields outside your house? And what if you turn on the floodlights and see unimaginable creatures battling in your fields? And what if your son and wife tell you you're the strange one because those fantastical creatures battling in your field are as natural as natural can be?

Follow Joseph's work in magazines and other anthologies at https://josephcarrabis.com/tag/im-published-here/

You can find most of Joseph's work at http://nlb.pub/amazon

About The Author

Joseph Carrabis told stories to anyone who would listen starting in childhood, wrote his first stories in gradeschool, and started getting paid for his writing in 1978. His work history includes periods as a long-haul trucker, apprentice butcher, apprentice coffee buyer/broker, lumberjack, Cold Regions researcher, mathematician, semanticist, semioticist, physicist, educator, Chief Data Scientist, Chief Research Scientist, and Chief Research Officer. He was an original member of the NYAS/UN's Scientists Without Borders program and held patents covering mathematics, anthropology, neuroscience, and linguistics. After patenting a technology he created in his basement and creating an international company, he retired from corporate life. Now he spends his time writing fiction based on his experiences. His work appears regularly in anthologies and his own novels. You can often find him playing with his dog, Boo, and snuggling with his wife, Susan. Learn more about him at https://josephcarrabis.com and his work at http://nlb.pub/amazon.

Did you enjoy *That Th!nk You Do*?

Please, write a review on Amazon http://nlb.pub/TTYDv1 and Goodreads http://nlb.pub/GTTYDv1 (and our thanks!)

You can find links to the blog posts mentioned in this book, as well as *That Th!nk You Do* trainings and contact info for Joseph to speak at your on- and off-line events at http://nlb.pub/TTYD

Become a member of Joseph's blog - josephcarrabis.com

Follow Joseph on
BookBub http://nlb.pub/BookBub
Facebook http://nlb.pub/Facebook
Goodreads http://nlb.pub/Goodreads
Instagram http://nlb.pub/Instagram
Linkedin http://nlb.pub/LinkedIn
Pinterest http://nlb.pub/Pinterest
Twitter http://nlb.pub/Twitter

www.ingramcontent.com/pod-product-compliance
Lightning Source LLC
Chambersburg PA
CBHW031416290426
44110CB00011B/404